Philosophy in Classrooms and Beyond

BIG IDEAS FOR YOUNG THINKERS

Thomas E. Wartenberg, Series Editor

The *Big Ideas for Young Thinkers* book series brings together the results of recent research about precollege philosophy. There has been sizable growth in philosophy programs for young people. The book series provides readers with a way to learn about all that is taking place in this important area of philosophical and educational practice. It brings together work from around the globe by some of the foremost practitioners of philosophy for children. The books in the series include single-author works as well as essay collections. With a premium placed on accessibility, the book series allows readers to discover the exciting world of precollege philosophy.

Philosophy in Classrooms and Beyond

New Approaches to Picture-Book Philosophy

Edited by
Thomas E. Wartenberg

ROWMAN & LITTLEFIELD
Lanham • Boulder • New York • London

Published by Rowman & Littlefield
An imprint of The Rowman & Littlefield Publishing Group, Inc.
4501 Forbes Boulevard, Suite 200, Lanham, Maryland 20706
www.rowman.com

6 Tinworth Street, London SE11 5AL, United Kingdom

Copyright © 2019 by Thomas E. Wartenberg

All rights reserved. No part of this book may be reproduced in any form or by any electronic or mechanical means, including information storage and retrieval systems, without written permission from the publisher, except by a reviewer who may quote passages in a review.

British Library Cataloguing in Publication Information Available

Library of Congress Cataloging-in-Publication Data

Names: Wartenberg, Thomas E., editor.
Title: Philosophy in classrooms and beyond : new approaches to picture-book philosophy / edited by Thomas E. Wartenberg.
Description: Lanham, Maryland : Rowman & Littlefield, [2019] | Series: Big ideas for young thinkers | Includes bibliographical references.
Identifiers: LCCN 2018053385 (print) | LCCN 2019004993 (ebook) | ISBN 9781475844597 (electronic) | ISBN 9781475844573 (cloth) | ISBN 9781475844580 (pbk.)
Subjects: LCSH: Philosophy—Study and teaching (Early childhood) | Children and philosophy.
Classification: LCC B52 (ebook) | LCC B52 .P5135 2019 (print) | DDC 372.8--dc23
LC record available at https://lccn.loc.gov/2018053385

Contents

List of Figures and Tables		vii
Foreword		ix
Roger Sutcliffe		
Preface: The Big Ideas for Little Kids Program		xiii
Introduction		xxiii
1	Bringing Undergraduates to Preschool: An Ethics Course for the Very Young *Erik Kenyon*	1
2	Restoring Wonder: The Benefits and Challenges of Doing Philosophy in Mixed-Aged Groups *Stephen Kekoa Miller*	17
3	Peace Building from Mali to Michigan *Stephen L. Esquith*	35
4	Helping Non-Philosophers Discuss Philosophy with Children: The Rotary Club Project *Ali Bassiri*	55
5	High School Goes to Kindergarten and Beyond *Mitchell Bickman and Laura Trongard*	67
6	The Promise and Challenge of Training College Students as Facilitators *Daniel Groll*	85
7	Picture Books Go to College: Introducing Philosophy to Undergraduates *Thomas E. Wartenberg*	103
List of Contributors		117

List of Figures and Tables

Table 1.1 A Complete Sequence of Lesson Arcs on Bravery	6
Table 1.2 Overview of a Fourteen-Week Term	9
Figure 3.1 Salif Happily Riding on the Back of His Father's Motorcycle. From *Camp Kati*.	45
Figure 3.2 The Chicken, the Bean, and the Worm Being Led to the *Taguna*. From *Building Peace*.	46
Figure 5.1 Rules Poster	71
Table 7.1 The Units of the Picture-Book Philosophy Course for First-Year College Students	109

Foreword
Roger Sutcliffe

The educational movement now generally referred to as P4C (Philosophy for Children) is fifty years old, having been conceived by Matthew Lipman, a professor at Columbia University, in 1968. It was, and remains, a conscious and concerted attempt to restore philosophy, or more precisely philosophical inquiry, to the heart of education proper.

During that half century, the movement has spread across the globe, and there are advocates and teachers of P4C in more than sixty countries.

With such a wide spread, over such a period of time, it should be no surprise that different approaches to this restoration have emerged. Not only has the original curriculum produced by Lipman and his associates at the IAPC (Institute for the Advancement of Philosophy for Children) been supplemented, or in some places supplanted, by other resources; but also there have been honorable suggestions of alternatives to labeling the movement "Philosophy for Children."

One, for example, recommends translating P4C as "Philosophy for Colleges," or even "Philosophy for Communities," to emphasize that the movement is not focused only on the education of young children. And for sure, its core practice, known as "Community of Inquiry," is valuable for students of all ages and in many contexts. This book makes that point very clearly.

Another suggested relabeling was PwC (Philosophy with Children), which was proposed partly to distinguish practice that did not use Lipman's materials, but partly to avoid the impression that P4C was a sort of condescending form of philosophy specially for children.

This label is still used respectfully and respectably. In fact, though, P4C was far from condescending in its conception, promoting as it did a vision of, and attitude toward, children that gave them more respect, especially as thinkers, than they had ever had. That is one of its abiding strengths.

Also, it is probably fair to say, the abbreviation P4C has proved very resilient, if only because it trips off the tongue fairly easily.

Whether or which, many people—including the editor of this book, Professor Tom Wartenberg—are happy to use the abbreviation, even while advocating and advancing practices (or practice areas) that Lipman may not have conceived of.

To say the latter is not, of course, to say that Lipman would have disapproved of them. Rather, I suspect, he would have been delighted at the varied collection of pioneering practices that this book reports on. It is evidence of the richness and sustainability of his vision—not only of children, but of the practice of philosophy itself.

Professor Wartenberg and his colleagues have shown how powerful philosophical inquiry can be as a driver, but also as a discipline, of good teaching and learning. Time and again in these reports there is a sense that engaging in open intellectual inquiry—in a way that is often neglected or even discouraged in many "learning" situations—reawakens in older participants the wonder and excitement that young children typically display as they experience and make sense of the world. As Professor Wartenberg himself says, "Big Kids deserve the chance to talk about Big Ideas just as much as little kids do."

And he admits that even he, who invented the Big Ideas Program primarily to introduce the excitement of philosophical inquiry to little kids, was inspired by his very program to try out new ideas and practices with his older students toward the end of his distinguished career at Mount Holyoke College.

The account he gives of his own experiments, in the final chapter of this book, provides a fascinating conclusion to the collection of other experiments, each of which pushed out the boundaries of P4C practice.

Perhaps none did this to quite the extent of the extraordinary—and extraordinarily brave—work of peace building in Mali, reported on in chapter 3. But each pioneer in his or her own setting showed the sort of professional courage and personal commitment from which we can all learn.

Several of the contributors noted the challenges they faced—and that would be faced by anyone who might be inspired by their reports to follow their examples. Those included:

- dealing with the anxiety or awkwardness of students trying to be honest in the company of older or younger people;
- countering the disrespect for children's voices that is endemic in test-oriented school cultures; managing overexpectations in cultures craving quick fixes; managing emotions in general that may be aroused by contentious, sometimes traumatic, issues;

- ensuring that the spirit of collaborative as well as critical inquiry was infused into family situations and relations—ironically, the greater challenge apparently arising in "more educated" families;
- teaching precollege or college students High Impact Practices that even college teachers do not always model;
- developing respectful and empathetic facilitation by high school students of kindergarten children, whom even elementary teachers sometimes struggle to understand;
- sensitively resolving the tension between the educational needs of college students and those of younger students.

But as well as identifying the various challenges, all the contributors steadily offered thoughtful and practical advice about how they could be met. Indeed, the careful deliberation they exhibited, and the descriptions and details they gave, spoke volumes of their professionalism.

And shining through the pages of the book are also the evidence and the excitement that P4C really does make a positive impact—well, many different positive impacts—on individuals and systems. It is for these examples and reasons that this book deserves to be read not only by P4C enthusiasts, but also by educators and managers in educational systems across the world.

Preface

The Big Ideas for Little Kids Program

Thomas E. Wartenberg

In the fall of 2000, a new course was offered by the Philosophy Department at Mount Holyoke College: Philosophy 280—Philosophy for Children. The course developed out of work I had done with children at a local elementary school, the Jackson Street School in Northampton, Massachusetts.

Because continuing to volunteer at the school seemed unsustainable, I decided that the best way to continue the school's philosophy program was to use undergraduate students to teach the elementary school philosophy sessions. This became the goal of the Big Ideas for Little Kids Program.

Since 2007, its philosophy classes have been offered at the Martin Luther King Jr. Charter School of Excellence in Springfield, Massachusetts, an inner-city school with an almost 100 percent minority population. Philosophy is now a standard part of the school's second-grade curriculum.

The Big Ideas for Little Kids Program attracted a great deal of attention, especially with the publication of *Big Ideas for Little Kids: Teaching Philosophy through Children's Literature*.

- The *New York Times* featured it in a story (www.nytimes.com/2010/04/18/edlife/18philosophy-t.html);
- its website, Teaching Children Philosophy—most of whose content is generated by students in Philosophy 280—is hugely popular (www.teachingchildrenphilosophy.org receives an average of thirty-four thousand visits a month);
- it was the subject of an award-winning PBS documentary, *Big Ideas for Little Kids* (streaming at www.wgby.org/bigideas);
- it has received a number of awards, including the 2011 Award for Excellence and Innovation in Philosophy Programs from the American Philosophical Association and Philosophy Distribution Center.

While all this recognition is immensely gratifying, there is an aspect of the program that was completely unexpected and that forms the basis for this book: Various people—college professors, high school teachers, parents, and community members—took the fundamental ideas behind the course, adopted some, and rejected others in order to create wonderfully innovative programs that go far beyond anything originally envisioned when Philosophy 280 was first conceived. These extraordinary programs are described by their originators in the chapters that compose this volume.

In this preface, the central ideas behind the Big Ideas for Little Kids Program will be outlined. This will give readers a context for understanding the innovations described in the book's subsequent chapters.

THE BIG IDEAS BEHIND THE BIG IDEAS FOR LITTLE KIDS PROGRAM

The first big idea that forms the basis of the Big Ideas for Little Kids Program is that children as young as six years old are actually interested in philosophical questions and have the ability to discuss them with insight and acumen. This flies in the face of much conventional wisdom about what children are capable of and what philosophy requires. Let's examine each of these conventional claims.

First, the claim that philosophy is not something children are capable of doing. You may be surprised to hear that I think that, on certain interpretations, this claim is valid. If what one means by philosophy is what professional philosophers in the United States generally do, e.g., participate in academic conferences and write journal articles, this is certainly not something young children can do.

More basically, if you take philosophy to require reading difficult texts, be they historical, such as René Descartes's *Meditations on First Philosophy*, or contemporary, such as John Rawls's *A Theory of Justice*, then children do not have many of the cognitive or emotional skills necessary for doing *that*. These are texts that present difficult and sustained arguments that young children simply cannot understand, even if they had the patience required to read or listen to them.

However, there is another, more fundamental conception of what the essence of philosophical activity is that children are quite capable of doing. I call this "the puzzle conception" of philosophy.

According to this understanding of philosophy, people encounter various *puzzles* in the course of living their lives. Some of these are intellectual, as when someone wonders if "the sky is real," since scientists tell us that there is nothing above us but various colorless gases that constitute the earth's atmosphere, so it doesn't appear that there is a blue object, the sky, above our heads as common sense suggests.

Others are more practical, as when someone sees another person drop a twenty-dollar bill and wonders whether it would be all right for them to pick it up and keep it rather than returning it to the person who dropped it. Although it may seem clear that they have a moral obligation to return the bill, is that still true if they have extreme need, such as to purchase medicine for a dying child and they lack the funds for doing that? In these dire circumstances, is it okay to keep the money?

Wrestling with these puzzling aspects of the world is what constitutes doing philosophy on the puzzle conception.

Philosophy has its roots in the puzzle conception. The Ancient Greek philosophers Plato and Aristotle support this view. Plato says that wonder is "the only beginning of philosophy" (Plato, *Theatetus* 155d). Now, one might think that this means that a philosopher begins in astonishment at certain miraculous features of the world, such as the starry heavens that excited Kant's wonder.

This is not the case, as Aristotle makes clear by associating wonder and perplexity:

> It is through wonder (*thaumazein*) that men now begin and originally began to philosophize; wondering in the first place at obvious perplexities (*atopōn*), and then by gradual progression raising questions about the greater matters too. (Aristotle, *Metaphysics* 1.2, 982b11–16)

Aristotle says that there are many features of the world and our experience of it that don't make sense when we reflect upon them, that perplex us, and these things cause us to wonder about them.

When we are puzzled (*aporōn*), Aristotle contends, we try to figure out what's true. According to Aristotle, that is the origin of philosophy, our being puzzled (*aporia*) about the world and our attempt to resolve that perplexity.

There are many aspects of children's lives that they find puzzling if not upsetting. I can recall my own son often saying, "but that's not fair," when he was told to do something he didn't want to do.

It might have been something as simple as going to bed when all the adults got to stay up. Rather than just telling him, "too bad," or something like that, there was the possibility of initiating a discussion of the nature of fairness and whether his claim was actually justified. Although that might not have been the most efficient way to get him into bed, the point remains that children use philosophical concepts and encounter philosophically rich situations simply in going about their daily lives.

For this reason, it makes sense to say that children are *natural-born philosophers*, as I have done, for children run up against philosophical puzzles in the normal course of their lives and struggle to resolve them. Unlike many adults, they are not yet prepared to brush aside those puzzles more or less unreflectively, accepting them as simply reflecting the way things are. Children demand to know *why* things are the way they are.

That's what makes them natural-born philosophers, for philosophy itself can be characterized as the intellectual discipline that, as Wilfrid Sellars (1962) put it, seeks "to understand how things in the broadest possible sense of the term hang together in the broadest sense of the term."

But you may immediately begin to doubt whether these youngsters are really capable of doing philosophy. After all, philosophy is a very abstract discipline, concerned with such concepts as morality and knowledge. Can young children really discuss these concepts in a philosophical manner?

The answer to this question will depend on what you mean by doing philosophy. But the crucial point to realize is that the core of philosophy, which is thinking in a careful and sustained manner about central issues arising in the course of living one's life, is certainly something children are capable of doing, especially when they are encouraged to do so *together* under the eyes of a watchful and sensitive adult.

This is precisely the goal of the Big Ideas for Little Kids Program: to assist young children in using their natural curiosity to engage with their peers in a sustained reflection on a question that puzzles them.

In order to accomplish this, the children need to learn to follow a simple set of rules that we formulate as imperatives:

- *Say* what you think in response to the question posed by the facilitator.
- *Listen* to what your classmate says.
- Figure out whether you *Agree or Disagree* with what was said.
- Provide a reason *Why* you think what you do.

These four "rules" are the basis of the so-called *SLAW* method that children need to internalize in order to have philosophical discussions with one another that are respectful even when there is vigorous disagreement. They form the basis of the philosophy lessons that constitute the class sessions for Philosophy 280.

Our elementary school philosophy sessions always begin with a "read aloud" in which the facilitator reads a picture book aloud to the children. We tried having the young students read the book aloud to their classmates but discovered that some of them were not comfortable doing so, which is why the facilitator does the read aloud. One of the benefits of this way of proceeding is that children love being read to and it's also a great way to get them to appreciate books.

Basing philosophy discussion on picture books is the second Big Idea underlying the Big Ideas for Little Kids Program. Initially, this was a pragmatic decision.

Elementary school teachers are already pressured to include a very wide variety of subjects in their classes, especially as a result of the rise of standardized testing. It therefore seemed unlikely they would respond in a positive manner to the request to include philosophy as a distinct subject among their other responsibilities such as teaching spelling, reading, math, and science.

However, teachers are required to use picture books to teach their students oral-language skills, a goal they often are unsure how to achieve. Once they understand philosophy lessons to be a way of helping students acquire these skills, they are much more likely to support the introduction of philosophy into their classroom.

But why, you may be wondering, are picture books an apt way to begin philosophy lessons? After all, picture books are entertaining and often very funny, a nice way to get kids to relax and go to sleep. Philosophy, on the other hand, is serious business, a discipline that has a reputation for difficulty and obscurity. The two seem ill-fitted for each other!

Aside from a basic misconception about philosophy (see above), this view misunderstands picture books. If we think about why children adore picture books, many features come to mind: Their rich illustrations and humorous narratives are certainly two factors. But an underappreciated factor in children's love of picture books is how they capture issues that children confront in their daily lives.

Take Maurice Sendak's classic *Where the Wild Things Are*. Certainly, its bold illustrations help account for its appeal. But an even more fundamental reason, I want to suggest, is the way in which it portrays the dialectic between powerlessness and power that young children frequently face in their lives.

Getting sent to bed without one's supper is a form of punishment that many children have endured. And many may have had fantasies of exercising disciplinary power themselves, even if not as cleverly and colorfully as Max. So, children can see in *Wild Things* their own experience, albeit in the distanced manner characteristic of works of art, thereby enabling them to reflect on the significance this issue has for their lives.

So far, a rationale for doing philosophy with elementary school children and a means of doing so have been addressed, but very little has been said about what is distinctive about the philosophical discussions that children have under our guidance. So, let's now turn to that issue.

One of the most important aspects of the Big Ideas for Little Kids Program is its departure from a standard model of teaching/education that conceives of the teacher as the possessor and dispenser of knowledge/wisdom to her ignorant charges. While there certainly is a place in education for providing knowledge to students who lack it, this is not something that is ever done in our work with elementary school children.

Instead of the teacher being the dispenser of knowledge, the alternatively dubbed *facilitator* functions as a type of umpire for the philosophical discussions that the young students engage in. In this role, the facilitator is prohibited from providing any substantive knowledge about the topic being discussed, functioning exclusively to assist the children in having a genuine discussion with one another. The ideal outcome of such a discussion is the generation of new ideas and perspectives, though consensus need not be achieved.

One feature of this alternative model of teaching is the removal of the teacher/facilitator from the center of the discussion. When the teacher is regarded as the dispenser of knowledge, she is the focus of the classroom, with students often vying with one another for her attention.

When the knowledgeable teacher is replaced with a skilled facilitator, the focus of the children's attention shifts from the teacher onto their classmates, for they need to listen carefully to one another and respond to what they have heard their classmates say. As a result, the classroom is transformed into what practitioners call "a community of inquiry," a term you will encounter often in this volume.

The term "community of inquiry" is one adopted from the American philosopher and originator of pragmatism, Charles Sanders Peirce. Peirce introduced that term to characterize the nature of scientific investigation. It replaced the older individualist model of the lone scientist boldly searching for the truth with a more accurate characterization of scientific research.

Peirce emphasized how scientists form a virtual community by interacting with each other to build the body of scientific knowledge. The scientist on this view is less like the individual painter working by herself to create a masterpiece than she is like one of the workers building a cathedral, for like a cathedral, science is the product of a joint undertaking of many individuals that proceeds over the course of many generations.

Applying this idea of an elementary school classroom emphasizes the possibility of knowledge being produced by children discussing issues together in a serious yet respectful manner analogous to how scientific inquiry is conducted. When children express their ideas, listen to what others say in a thoughtful yet critical manner, and express their agreements and disagreements thoughtfully using reasons that can themselves become the subject of critical discussion, they have the capacity for deep and innovative philosophical thinking.

Facilitating such discussions is no easy matter, for the facilitator must pay close attention to what the children say and figure out how to use their comments to focus on a relevant philosophical issue. Many different skills go into making a successful facilitator, including the ability to think on one's feet and to see when a comment raises a genuine philosophical issue the students would do well to discuss together.

The discussions directed by a skilled facilitator not only help the children develop interesting and often innovative ideas, they build strong bonds among the students who come to see themselves as working together even when they disagree with one another about specific issues. Just as in science, disagreement is often the catalyst for the creation of new ideas and theories in an elementary school philosophy discussion. So, disagreement is something that is fostered in a philosophical classroom so long as it is conducted in a civil and respectful manner.

The final Big Idea I shall discuss in this preface is one of the most innovative features of the Big Ideas for Little Kids Program: its use of undergraduate college students as facilitators of elementary school philosophy discussions.

Initially, as with the choice of prompts for the philosophy lessons, this was a pragmatic decision. Undergraduates provided a ready resource for philosophy teaching. As a college professor, I had a regular schedule of classes, and dedicating one to teaching philosophy in elementary schools seemed an easy way to get philosophy lessons into more classrooms than I could manage as a single volunteer in a school.

Over time, the wisdom of this strategy was confirmed. Not only did the college students enjoy teaching the elementary school pupils, along the way they learned a great deal of philosophy. After all, the conventional wisdom is that one only really learns a subject by teaching it. So why not give undergraduates the opportunity to do just that?

In addition, the elementary school kids *loved* being taught by college students. The attention shown them by the college students, who asked them *what they thought* and then listened very carefully to what they had to say, was something that the young children really appreciated. This led them to try very hard to do exactly what the college students requested that they do, namely, engage in a philosophy discussion that proceeds according to the SLAW method.

There certainly are problems with using college students as philosophical facilitators. First, many of them do not have much experience working with young children. This makes it somewhat difficult for them to relate to a group of often unruly kids in a classroom.

In addition, many of them do not have a good background in philosophy, making it difficult for them to know how to respond to the often-challenging comments that young children make during a discussion. Finally, being a teacher is a new experience for most undergraduates, one that makes them quite nervous. As a result, it is hard for them to focus on the discussion that is taking place rather than worry about what their next intervention will be.

None of these problems is insurmountable, but they indicate the challenges faced by anyone wanting to use undergraduates as philosophical facilitators. Clearly, having an effective means of teaching undergraduates how to teach philosophy is necessary for any course using undergraduate facilitators.

The challenging nature of providing such training is not a reason to resist using college students as facilitators of elementary school philosophy discussions. It should be a warning that doing so requires careful planning of the instruction that the college students receive for teaching philosophy to elementary school children.

And undergraduates are not the only ones who pose problems as facilitators of philosophy lessons. Community members and teachers with little or no philosophical training have been used to teach philosophy in some of the programs discussed in this volume.

Each of these groups pose unique challenges, for despite their ability to work well with children, they often lack any philosophical training. This makes it more difficult for them to know how to make a discussion based on picture books turn into a vibrant philosophical one.

A discussion that remains focused on the story without any movement toward a more abstract issue will not be a genuine philosophy discussion. To achieve such a discussion, facilitators need to have some knowledge of philosophy.

If one has the goal of spreading philosophy into elementary school classrooms, great creativity is certainly required. While one solution is to train teachers to lead philosophy discussions, at least in the United States this hasn't been possible on a wide scale.

This is one reason why the work inspired by the Big Ideas for Little Kids Program is so important: It shows some of the incredibly creative ideas people have had for introducing philosophy into new and unexpected contexts, many of them involving young children but not all. Although the focus of this book is introducing young children to philosophy, its ambitions are broader, for its wider aim is taking philosophy into many contexts where it can be useful, if only people recognize the importance of doing so.

The Big Ideas for Little Kids Program has been successful both in its own right and as a result of the programs it has inspired. But this book is not intended as a celebration of the program and its "offspring." Rather, it is meant to suggest the wide range of possibilities that exist for bringing philosophy to young people and, indeed, many others. Readers are encouraged to use their own creativity to develop new ways of incorporating philosophy into the lives of young children—and others.

REFERENCES

Descartes, René. 2017. *Meditations on First Philosophy*. Translated by John Cottingham. Cambridge, UK: Cambridge University Press.
Peirce, Charles Sanders. 1877. "The Fixation of Belief." https://en.wikisource.org/wiki/The_Fixation_of_Belief. Accessed June 9, 2018.
Plato. 1967. *Theatetus, Sophist*. Translated by Harold North Fowler. Cambridge, MA: Harvard University Press.
Rawls, John. *A Theory of Justice*. Cambridge, MA: Harvard University Press.
Sellars, Wilfrid S. 1962. "Philosophy and the Scientific Image of Man." In *Science, Perception, and Reality*, edited by Robert Colodny, 35–78. New York: Humanities Press / Ridgeview.
Wartenberg, Thomas. 2014. *Big Ideas for Little Kids: Teaching Philosophy through Children's Literature*. 2nd edition. Lanham, MD: Rowman & Littlefield.

[illegible]

REFERENCES

[illegible]

Introduction
Thomas E. Wartenberg

The various contributions to this book discuss a variety of programs that have been influenced by the Big Ideas for Little Kids Program. All of the creators of these programs have picked and chosen among the program's Big Ideas to develop their own innovative programs. While Philosophy 280: Philosophy for Children is the inspiration behind this diverse set of initiatives, they each go beyond that course to develop innovative means of bringing philosophy into spaces where it had not previously been.

This introduction contains capsule summaries of each chapter of this book. The individual chapters each describe one of the diverse programs inspired by Big Ideas for Little Kids.

In his contribution, "Bringing Undergraduates to Preschool: An Ethics Course for the Very Young," Erik Kenyon details the benefits and difficulties of having undergraduates teach philosophy in a preschool setting. Preschool children have much shorter attention spans than elementary school children, and that results in formidable difficulties confronting someone trying to introduce philosophy into early childhood classrooms.

Kenyon has developed a program at Rollins College that does just that, but in so doing he has had to expand the methods used in elementary school classrooms to include games and art projects. His chapter details these changes and makes suggestions about how such a course could be implemented by others.

Stephen Kekoa Miller began his program by having high school children teach philosophy to younger students in the school at which he teaches. But over time, he modified his approach to include graduates of the school and other interested adults.

As he describes the program in "Restoring Wonder: The Benefits and Challenges of Doing Philosophy in Mixed-Aged Groups," Miller reflects on the impact that the community of inquiry method has on those taking part in philosophical discussions. Bringing together ideas from a wide range of sources, Miller ties his philosophy program into the tradition of philosophy going back to the Ancient Greeks.

The program that departs to the greatest extent from the model suggested by the Big Ideas for Little Kids Program is described by Stephen L. Esquith in "Peace Building from Mali to Michigan." Although Esquith began by introducing a philosophy-for-children course at Michigan State University, with the assistance of his own students he built a unique and innovative program in Mali.

One of the unique features of this program is that schoolteachers actually create their own picture books that are then produced using traditional cloth-making techniques. Some of the pages of these books are reproduced in his chapter. Esquith suggests that the methods he has developed play an important role in peace building, a process that is crucial to the future of a country suffering the effects of widespread violence and terror.

When Ali Bassiri contacted me with his idea of using the members of his Rotary Club to teach philosophy in local schools, I was skeptical. I just wasn't sure that the members of that organization possessed the requisite knowledge and skills. But I was wrong, as Bassiri demonstrates in "Helping Non-Philosophers Discuss Philosophy with Children: The Rotary Club Project."

For a number of years, Bassiri and his fellow Rotarians taught philosophy in two elementary schools, one public and one private. Surprisingly, Bassiri found that the public school teachers were more amenable to adopting the community of inquiry methodology that is integral to elementary school philosophy. His use of a group of committed adults to develop his program suggests that there may be opportunities to reach out to many unexpected groups to increase the number of philosophy programs for young children.

In terms of its reach, Mitchell Bickman and Laura Trongard's program is exemplary. As they describe in "High School Goes to Kindergarten and Beyond," in only a few years their program of using high school students to teach philosophy in kindergarten has blossomed from a small pilot program into one in which philosophy has been introduced into all the elementary school grades. Over 350 high school students have been trained as facilitators and over two thousand young children have participated in philosophy lessons. All this in only four years!

Aside from this astronomical growth, Bickman and Trongard detail how they train their high school facilitators to work with young children and what their sessions look like. If such a program were replicated, think of how many students—both in elementary school and high school—could be taught philosophy!

In "The Promise and Challenge of Training College Students as Facilitators," Daniel Groll provides an extensive discussion of problems that face anyone trying to use college students as facilitators of elementary school philosophy discussions. These issues arise in part because the goals for the course conflict with one another.

Although it's clear that the central aim of the course is to have good discussions at the elementary school level and this entails training the college students to be able to do so, they are also taking a college-level philosophy course. To be true to this aspect of the course, they have to think about the issues the young students will discuss at a level characteristic of college philosophy courses. Groll discusses the tension that arises from trying to achieve both aims in a course that is taught in only one term.

The book's final chapter describes an introduction to philosophy course for undergraduate students that is based on picture books. This course was inspired by the excitement that reading picture books generated among elementary school students and was an experiment to see if college students would also find picture books a useful stimulus for philosophical discussions.

The chapter gives a detailed explanation of how the course was structured and assesses its strengths and weaknesses. It shows that the work done in teaching philosophy to young children can be used to develop innovations in higher education.

That philosophy can be an important part of the lives of every human being is the unspoken assumption behind the desire shared by all the contributors of this volume to bring philosophy into contexts where it has not previously existed. This belief explains the efforts they have made to develop innovative philosophy programs.

As well as being a record of a range of extraordinary programs, this volume is also meant to inspire others to take up the mantle of advocate for philosophy and strive to expand the audience for philosophy in a manner that suits their particular situation. The contributors to this volume will then serve as role models as individuals who have developed novel means for bringing philosophy to a wider public.

Chapter One

Bringing Undergraduates to Preschool
An Ethics Course for the Very Young
Erik Kenyon

Big Ideas for Little Kids (Wartenberg 2014) grew out of a course Tom Wartenberg developed at Mount Holyoke College. In sending undergraduates to work with elementary school students at local public schools, this course provides a powerful model in the Philosophy for Children (P4C) movement, which benefits elementary school children and undergraduates alike. Similar courses at Rollins College, in partnership with five Orlando-area schools, have distilled and adapted Wartenberg's methods for use with children as young as four years old.

Led by Erik Kenyon, in close collaboration with Diane Terorde-Doyle, director of Rollins's Child Development and Student Research Center, these courses have filled various functions in Rollins's General Education curriculum, all at the Introductory level. This approach helps students new to philosophy learn material by applying it through lessons with children and could easily be adapted for high school, and perhaps even middle school,[1] students as well.

The present chapter takes as its model for discussion a pre-K P4C project in the context of an undergraduate first-year seminar. The first half of the chapter lays out *how* to build such a course, using *Big Ideas's* methods as a point of departure and laying out considerations necessary for aligning learning goals of older "students" and younger "children."[2] The second half addresses *why* to build such a course, setting out rationales for extending *Big Ideas'* basic project to include even younger children and looking to students' learning outcomes, which embody several best practices of liberal education.[3]

FROM DISCUSSION FRAMEWORK TO LESSON ARC

Big Ideas avoids approaching P4C in terms of "lesson plans," which can descend into rigid lists of what to cover when. Instead, it presents a "discussion framework," which sets parameters for discussions and then allows children to take things where they will. This is a valuable "learner-centered" corrective to the "teacher-centered," content-laden approach dominant in America's schools today. The particulars of *Big Ideas's* discussion frameworks, however, were developed with elementary school children in mind. As they stand, they are too demanding for the concrete thinking and shorter attention spans of pre-K children.[4]

A *Big Ideas* discussion framework begins with reading a picture book aloud. A "story matrix" follows, as students walk children through philosophically salient points of a story, filling out a chart as they go. This primes children for philosophically rich "discussion questions" that spark conversation between children, whose interactions are guided by a set of nine philosophy rules. The lesson concludes with a "go around" as each child reflects on the session and shares with the group what he or she found most valuable or surprising about it.

When working with pre-K children, this approach must be altered rather drastically. The storybook remains the linchpin of this altered method, yet it is situated in a broader set of activities referred to as a "lesson arc."

Rather than jump straight into reading a storybook, students open with a game to focus children on philosophically salient details of that story. Before discussing moderation in the *Frog and Toad Forever* story "Cookies," for instance, students may help children mix paint, divvying out colors, each time asking children: Is this *too little* blue? Is this *too much* red? Is this purple *just right*? By the end of the game, children have a working vocabulary of moderation, excess, and deficiency at the front of their minds.

Rather than follow a storybook reading with a story matrix, the two can be combined as students pause periodically *during* the reading for a series of mini-discussions. In the case of "Cookies," students might pause to ask: If eating cookies is fun, how can you tell when you've had too many? Dialogical reading, which has long standing in early education circles, is here put to philosophical use, as it is less taxing on young children who lack the attention span and reading abilities that the *Big Ideas* story matrix requires.

Discussion questions, rather than being presented to children sitting in a circle, become prompts for art projects. This approach to scaffolding through art owes much to the Reggio Emilia tradition (Hertzog 2001) and gives children something tangible to help structure discussion of open-ended questions. In the "Cookies" case, the college students may bring back the colors children have mixed, give children paper plates, and ask them to paint their perfect meal. The goal is to engage children while, not after, they work: What's on your plate? Are you really going to eat three plates of food? Logan only wants one plate; why do you think that is?[5]

While *Big Ideas* calls on children to sit still and discuss ideas for protracted periods, this more embodied approach is developmentally appropriate for the concrete thinking of younger children. The result is a chatty kind of chaos as games, storybooks, and art projects spark a series of mini-discussions between children and students. Its frequent shifts in activities also serve to reset children's attention clock, expanding the length of useful discussion time and even allowing students to pursue parts of lesson arcs over the course of multiple days.

PRACTICING THE PHILOSOPHY RULES

Big Ideas presents philosophy as a type of game, governed by a set of nine rules. This clarifies what is expected of children in philosophy sessions and presents the essence of what philosophers *do* in a way that translates easily into elementary school classrooms. For work with pre-K, these rules may be distilled to three: we listen, we think, we respond. They must also be taught and practiced in developmentally appropriate ways.

New research into executive function has revived interest in games such as *Red Light Green Light*, which help children develop that inner "pause" button (Kenyon and Terorde-Doyle 2017a). The point of the listening rule is to make sure that children are paying attention to what others are actually saying. You might practice this with a game of *Telephone* or *Simon Says*, repeating the injunction to "listen" along the way.

The thinking rule calls on children to consider their own ideas *before* responding: What does the other person think? Do I think the same or something different? This is cognitively demanding for a young child. *Charades* can help them think about thinking. You may, for instance, ask a child to act out the scariest animal there is. As that child decides on an animal, you can draw the others' attention to the fact that s/he is thinking. As the first child acts out that animal, you may ask the children to "think" about what animal they are seeing. These acts of metacognition help children understand *what* you're asking when you tell them to "think."

The kind of thinking we're asking of children is wrapped up in position taking, which bleeds into the responding rule. To practice, students provide verbal scaffolding, e.g., "Alice, say, 'I disagree with you, Ben, because . . .'" You might practice this with the *River Game*. For this, roll out a paper river on the floor and ask for one child's view on a particular question, e.g., what is the best pet? Those who agree with that child stand on his/her side of the river; those who disagree stand on the other side. According to Piaget, the egocentrism of very young children renders them unable to see the world from others' perspectives. In reality, it just takes practice.[6]

The first few times playing the *River Game*, the older students will likely have to explain the implications of where children are standing: "Charlie, you think that cats are the best pet, but Donna doesn't think that. She's standing over there because she thinks that turtles are the best pet. Do you want to say why you disagree with Donna?" While "What is the best pet?" is perhaps not the most philosophical question, seeing things from multiple perspectives is good practice for more substantial philosophical disagreements. Once they get into the habit of saying, "I agree/disagree with you because . . ." things take off.[7]

PHILOSOPHICAL PUZZLES

The point of these rules is to foster a certain kind of discussion, in which children take positions relative to each other, articulate reasons for those positions, and at times change those positions based on what others have to say. All of this requires embracing disagreement in ways that run counter to the culture of many American schools.

Teachers often see getting everyone on the same page as fundamental to classroom management. When conflict comes up, many teachers seem hardwired to seek a consensus or, at least, to get children "to agree to disagree." Testing practices reinforce this: AP assessors do not look favorably on those who question the AP version of history, write in a form other than the five-paragraph essay, or otherwise "color outside the lines." As a result, students today tend not to be very good at disagreeing. This is a major obstacle to running a P4C project.

Students are, of course, familiar with disagreements, but mostly from the world of politics, which has descended into a form of tribalism: Liberals think X; conservatives think Y. The result, from a philosophical perspective, is that students arrive at college with two gears, absolutism and relativism, which they will flip-flop between with little rhyme or reason.

This comes out when the college students are called on to write lesson arcs. At times, they engage in what sometimes passes today as "Socratic method," i.e., assuming the right answer but then not telling children what it is. At other times, they swing to the opposite extreme and ask about mere matters of opinion. In the classroom, the one approach quickly descends into a fishing trip, as the students look for children to give the "right answer"; the other becomes little more than show and tell: If children are merely expressing opinions, there is nothing really to disagree about. In neither case is real philosophical progress possible.

The Ancients' concept of a philosophical puzzle, *aporia*, can help move students beyond this impasse. In Plato's Socratic dialogues, the term tends to mean "perplexity" or "being at a loss" (the literal meaning is "having no way forward"). In Aristotle's hands, it means something more like a "puzzle" or "thorny question to be resolved." In either case, it denotes a real problem arising from lived experience, about which there can be real and useful disagreement.

In more modern terms, you might think of this as a "pluralist" question. If an absolutist question (e.g., "why do some rocks float?") has one right answer and a relativist question has as many right answers as there are individuals or cultures answering it (e.g., "what is your favorite color?") then a pluralist question has more than one viable answer but does not permit an "anything goes" response. For example, what makes an action right or wrong? Consequences, intent, God's will, my values, a social contract. . . . Any professional philosopher could come up with a number of viable responses, yet that number will probably not exceed five or ten.

Questions that walk this middle way provide a real starting point for philosophical discussion. The best of them are the sort that people have to take *some* stance on simply to get through a day. Students need practice asking such questions. "What would Aristotle do with this storybook?" is a good place to start.

The following checklist can help students articulate philosophical puzzles for use with children: Does your question . . .

- ✓ matter to children / connect with their everyday experience?
- ✓ have no single, clearly agreed upon answer?
- ✓ not invite mere opinion or an "anything goes" response?
- ✓ need to be answered in some way, at least provisionally, to get through a day?

Such questions are the heart of philosophical discussions.

Beyond the demands of a P4C project or the subject matter of a philosophy course, the ability to articulate questions will serve college students well in other courses and life beyond college. Such questions provide a framework for working through disagreements, clarifying positions, seeking reasons, and refining issues. If "critical thinking" is a generally desirable learning outcome, then philosophers are uniquely well suited to contribute to it by helping students ask better, more useful questions.

BUILDING A COURSE FOR CHILDREN

Philosophy pushes children to the edge of their ability to verbalize ideas. There are times when you can almost "see" the wheels turning behind their eyes, as they struggle to wrap words around new ideas. This takes time. It is best to come back to each central idea—courage, friendship, fairness—in two to four different lesson arcs, each one approaching the matter from a slightly different angle. A complete sequence on bravery is presented in table 1.1.[8]

This material could easily be spread across three weeks by playing games on Tuesdays and returning Thursdays for storybooks and art projects. Giving time between activities allows ideas to simmer beneath the surface (children often think like slow cookers). Students sometimes find this distressing, as they have spent years learning new material, getting tested on it, and then moving on. Working with pre-K children invites students to step back, slow down, and think about what authentic learning looks like.

The speed with which a group of children will "get it" depends on a whole host of factors. It's best to play it by ear, adding or taking away activities as useful. If possible, lesson arcs should be arranged so that the opening games cycle through practicing different rules. Given that students spend a relatively short amount of time with children, the more time the school's teaching staff can take to reinforce the philosophy rules, the better.

Children experience the project as visits from students who take part in typical pre-K activities but, as one child put it, "sure do ask a lot of ques-

Table 1.1. A Complete Sequence of Lesson Arcs on Bravery

	Puzzle	Game (Rule Practiced)	Storybook	Art Project
1	Looking Brave vs. Being Brave	River Game: "Which princess/ superhero doll is bravest?" (Respond)	Robert Munsch, *Paper Bag Princess*	Roleplay: How does each doll respond to dangerous scenarios? Is he/she brave?
2	Brave vs. Afraid	Lead children around blindfolded. (Listen)	Arnold Lobel, "Dragons & Giants"	Draw a time you were scared. Were you brave?
3	Brave vs. Reckless	Charades: Act out a scary animal. (Think)	Kevin Henkes, *Sheila Rea the Brave*	Draw something reckless you did. Were you brave?

tions." Over time, children come to imitate students' questioning. The vocabulary of the lessons also makes its way onto the playground, "Look at me on the slide; I'm being brave" or "you need to use more self-control," as do the phrases "I agree" and "I disagree." In the end, the project gives children license to express their own ideas and the skills to explore them through discussions with others.

BUILDING A COURSE FOR STUDENTS

The instructor's role is to introduce students to new material and to support them as they design, implement, and reflect on lessons arcs for the children. Like comedy, this is mostly a matter of timing. The instructor's task is to align the learning curves of students who may have no background in philosophy or early education, and that of pre-K children, who learn best by approaching subjects in short meetings, multiple times, from slightly different angles.

This requires narrowing the range of philosophical material covered. *Big Ideas* reflects an Introductory Philosophy Survey Course, covering nine areas from Logic to Environmental Philosophy. Its counterpart at Rollins reflects an Introduction to Ethical Theory. Staying within a single subject area in philosophy allows children to move at a developmentally appropriate pace.[9] Questions from ethics, in turn, resonate well with the challenges and preoccupations of both pre-K and undergraduate life.

The first half of term introduces students to the course's "first-order" content, ethical theory, in typical ways (readings, discussions, papers). Students spend the second half of the term working with children and exploring philosophy of education as a way to reflect on that work. This "second-order" thinking about thinking, in turn, provides a mirror for students to reflect on their own education: How did this discussion with the four-year-olds go? How could it go better? What makes something a *good* discussion? What is the point of discussing ideas? What am *I* looking for out of my courses? How am I contributing to them?

Students experience the course as a move from being challenged in their values and exploring theoretical frameworks to applying these frameworks in lessons with children and taking a critical perspective on education in ever more self-reflective ways. In their final assignment, students draw these threads together by writing a letter to themselves on the day of their college graduation. In this, they use materials from the course to reflect on their education thus far and talk about what they hope to accomplish in their time at college and beyond.

CRAFTING A SCHEDULE

How can you fit all this into a single term, you ask? Ideally, travel and site visits can be built into course time. At Rollins, that means meeting Tuesdays and Thursdays in seventy-five-minute blocks. If the class covers one lesson arc with children per week, then six weeks of site visits work as a minimum plus an initial "playdate," allowing students and children to get comfortable with each other. If you leave a workshop week in the middle of your visits to regroup (see below), then the playdate is set on week seven of a fourteen-week term. In other words, you spend the second half of term on-site, as students split their time between class and work with children.

This can be sliced up in various ways, depending on travel time and resources. All three of the following have been used in courses at Rollins:

a) All students spend Tuesdays in class and Thursdays working with children.
b) Half of the students spend Tuesdays in class, while the other half spend Tuesdays working with children. On Thursdays, the two groups switch roles.
c) All students spend the first portion of each day's class time in class and the rest traveling to and from the school where they work with children for fifteen minutes on Tuesdays and twenty to twenty-five minutes on Thursdays.

The rest is an exercise in staggering deadlines. If students are placed in groups of three, then each of them gets to write lesson arcs and lead discussions twice in the span of six weeks. For this to work, the first batch of lesson arcs must be ready by week eight and the second batch by week twelve. Once work starts on-site, the rate at which material is covered is cut in half. In practice, this leaves roughly the last third of term, starting around week eleven, for thinking about philosophy of education. Putting this all together, and weaving in readings from *Big Ideas* to help students prepare for work with children, produces the type of curriculum illustrated in table 1.2.[10]

WHY WORK WITH PRE-K CHILDREN?

America's pre-K schools, and kindergartens to a large extent, are relatively free from the crushing regime of testing that has descended on grade schools, whether public or independent. Perhaps as a result, pre-K teachers have developed their own distinctive culture, which tends to be more flexible, more improvisatory and more open to trying new things. Is that to say that we should focus our efforts on pre-K rather than higher grades? Not at all!

Table 1.2. Overview of a Fourteen-Week Term

Week	Tuesday	Thursday
1	Plato, *Euthyphro*	Plato, *Apology*
2	Aristotle, EN 1.4, 5, 7, 8 (flourishing)	Aristotle, EN 2 (habit); 3.6–9 (bravery)
3	Aristotle, EN 3.10–12; 7.1–3 (moderation); Epictetus, *Handbook*	Aristotle, EN 8.1–3; 9.8–9 (friendship); 10.6–8 (study)
4	Peer Review Workshop: Essay 1 on Aristotle; Visit from Career Center	Mill, *Utilitarianism* 1; *Big Ideas*, chs. 3–4; Kenyon and Doyle, "Three R's of Thinking"
5	Mill, *Utilitarianism* 2 (first half); *Big Ideas*, ch. 5	Mill, *Utilitarianism* 2 (second half); "Singer Solution"; Epicurus, *Letters*; *Big Ideas*, ch. 6
6	Kant, *Groundwork*, Preface; Kenyon and Doyle, "Art & Dialogue"	Kant, *Groundwork*, Section 1
7	Workshop on First Batch of Lesson Arcs; *Big Ideas*, chs. 7–8	Playdate; Revised Essay 1 Due
8	Use Lesson Arc 1 (Ancient Ethics); Revised Lesson Arcs Due	Kant, *Groundwork*, Section 2 (first half)
9	Use Lesson Arc 2 (Ancient Ethics)	Kant, *Groundwork*, Section 2 (second half)
10	Use Lesson Arc 3 (Ancient Ethics)	Peer Review Workshop: Essay 2 on Kant and/or Mill
11	American Pragmatism: John Dewey	Workshop on Second Batch of Lesson Arcs; Readings on Reggio Emilia
12	Use Lesson Arc 4 (Modern Ethics); Revised Lesson Arcs Due	Pragmatism at Rollins: Hamilton Holt
13	Use Lesson Arc 5 (Modern Ethics); Revised Essay 2 Due	Black Mountain College: Andrew Rice
14	Use Lesson Arc 6 (Modern Ethics); Draft of Final Projects	Rollins Today: Grant Cornwell
Finals	Letter to Future Self and Internship Application	

There is every indication that the best scenario is to integrate philosophical methods into instruction as early and as often as possible. Many contributors to this collection present innovative ways of improving the existing K12 system. The present point is simply that "as early as possible" is in fact earlier than many P4C practitioners have assumed. Meanwhile, colleges and high schools looking to establish ongoing partnerships with schools for younger children may find it easiest to find openings in preschool schedules.

Through P4C programs, pre-K children become more confident in holding and expressing their own views. Such programs also help expand the scope of "teachable moments" that pre-K teachers see cropping up in the course of a day, as hurt feelings and arguments over toys become opportunities to think about fairness or moderation. Teachers at Rollins's partner schools have continued in this spirit, introducing discussions of new ideas, such as mindfulness and international relations, into their pre-K classes.

HOW DO STUDENTS BENEFIT FROM TEACHING CHILDREN PHILOSOPHY?

Given that P4C is a form of community service, it is perhaps easiest to see children as the main beneficiaries of the project. Yet what exactly do students get out of such work? The American Association of Colleges and Universities (AAC&U) has produced a list of ten High Impact Practices (HIPs), which have been shown to improve student learning, engagement, and retention (AAC&U n.d.):

First-Year Seminars
Common Intellectual Experiences
Learning Communities
Writing-Intensive Courses
Collaborative Assignments/Projects

Undergraduate Research
Diversity / Global Learning
Community-Based Learning
Internships
Capstone Courses and Projects

While this list, and the research it rests on, focuses on undergraduates, many elements of it translate easily to secondary education as well. Research shows that any one of these HIPs will improve student learning (Kuh 2008). What's more, their effect is cumulative: The more HIPs a student encounters, the more learning improves.

Administrators at leading schools are eager to weave HIPs into their curricula. Putting any one of these into practice, however, requires considerable planning. The call for *several* is enough to make most faculty simply throw up their hands. The way for faculty to give administrators what they want and students what they need is to find a single goal to which multiple HIPs provide the means, in this case: Helping a group of four-year-olds develop skills necessary to engage in philosophical discussions of ethical questions.[11] Rollins's P4C first-year seminar incorporates at least five HIPs in ways that are meaningful and sustainable.[12]

Community-Based Learning invites students to develop real-world problem-solving skills by working through real-world problems. But there is something inherently unsustainable here. In preparing a course, faculty must find a community partner, identify a project, and develop assignments to allow students and community partners to work together on that project. Yet if the project is successfully completed at the end of term, the instructor, who has already put in considerable preparation time, must start the process all over again.

Such projects take many forms. At Rollins, courses in professional writing have partnered with nonprofit agencies to develop website content. A human resources course has partnered with local healthcare providers to identify inefficiencies and propose solutions. A course in computer science has worked with the historical society of a local neighborhood to develop a walking-tour app. While each project was meaningful to students and helpful to community partners, they left instructors having to seek out new projects and new partners each term.

Problems with America's K12 system run deep and are not going away anytime soon. Schools staggering under the weight of standardized testing are producing a population that is increasingly ill-prepared to engage in the critical thinking and civic discourse required by twenty-first-century life. While this is not the root cause of all our problems, the United States' standing challenges—racism, nationalism, mass shootings, a failing healthcare system, the refusal to address environmental crises—are all perpetuated by political polarization, which is, in turn, perpetuated by the American people's increasing inability to engage in useful dialogue with those across the aisle.

These problems are much too extensive to be solved by a one-term college course. A class can, however, chip away at them, by addressing the more tractable problem: How can a group of students help a group of children practice skills of critical thinking and useful dialogue? This is a problem that can be addressed in a term. What's more, it is sustainable, as the cyclical nature of the school year keeps bringing fresh batches of children to work with.

P4C employs *Collaborative Assignments/Projects* in a couple of respects. A typical student cannot manage a group of four-year-olds alone. Students are thus placed in groups of three or four to work with groups of eight to twelve children each. Each student, in turn, develops and leads at least one lesson arc with the assistance of his or her peers. All students are then required to write "site reports" on all lessons, regardless of who the leader is, and groups are given class time at key points in the term to coordinate topics and tweak strategies as problems arise.[13]

This approach to P4C provides another form of collaboration: between students and children. The AAC&U lists one of the main goals of group work, as "sharpening one's own understanding by listening seriously to the insights of others, especially those with different backgrounds and life experiences" (AAC&U n.d.). P4C work with pre-K children provides ample opportunities for this.[14]

This brings us to a third HIP: *Diversity / Global Learning*. Rollins's P4C program routinely partners with Winter Park Day Nursery, a voluntary pre-K serving a diverse group of families from socioeconomic backgrounds different than those of most Rollins students. Children's unfiltered reports of their experiences are often eye-opening for students. Beyond the particulars of the schools involved, however, young children constitute a class of people whose views are routinely ignored by U.S. society.

Add to this the challenges posed by four-year-olds' still developing grasp of English, and students are given ample opportunity to practice engaging in meaningful discussions across cultural and linguistic barriers. If you can meaningfully discuss Kant's ideas with a four-year-old, you know what you're talking about. While Rollins's P4C project does not directly explore issues of racial, cultural, political, or religious diversity, the philosophy rules it teaches—listen, think, respond—provide children and students alike with the foundational skills for bridging divides.

Rollins's P4C program is also an ongoing pedagogical experiment. In certain semesters, students have been called on to compose lesson arcs *rather than* write traditional philosophy papers. The result was mediocre. Students generally found some idea to latch on to, but they had a poor grasp of alternative perspectives and how they relate to one another. In retrospect, the better approach is to integrate, rather than oppose, traditional essay writing with more experimental approaches to learning through writing lesson plans.

Writing-Intensive Courses, particularly when that writing is philosophical, help students develop skills in navigating complex and ambiguous issues. To critique Aristotle's account of friendship or analyze an ethical dilemma from competing perspectives, students must break complicated ideas into their component parts, situate ideas in "conceptual space," draw connections, take positions, and give reasons for them. This prepares them to think on their feet, which is exactly what they need to work with the unpredictable things children will say.

The writing process is woven through the entire course, starting as students post questions online based on the night's readings. Through in-class discussions, they develop these into essay topics and write essay outlines. Students then write drafts, provide comments on the substance of each other's drafts through a peer-review exercise, and then respond to their peers by name in their final drafts.[15] This helps students practice thinking within a community: seeing themselves as occupying particular positions in "logical space" and relating to others through agreements, disagreements, and individuals' various reasons for them.

P4C courses at Rollins have filled various functions within the General Education curricula: humanities, critical thinking, ethical reasoning, intro to the liberal arts. The self-reflective nature of P4C courses and their critical exploration of education, however, make them ideally suited for use as

First-Year Seminars. As the AAC&U has it, "The highest-quality first-year experiences place a strong emphasis on critical inquiry, frequent writing, information literacy, collaborative learning, and other skills that develop students' intellectual and practical competencies" (AAC&U n.d.).

This form of active reflection on students' educational goals is useful for students at any critical juncture. Working with more advanced undergraduates at Tufts, Susan Russinoff reports:

> During the semester, philosophy majors commented that thinking about designing the lesson plans and then delivering them made them think more fundamentally about their own study of philosophy and its value. One senior major commented that the work with children and the way it made him think differently about philosophical questions and discourse was a perfect way for him to end his four years of philosophy study at Tufts. (Email to author, June 21, 2018.)

A recent addition to the AAC&U's list of HIPs, which has not been used at Rollins, is the *ePortfolio*. As top schools move away from traditional quizzes and testing and into more project-based courses, "ePortfolios enable students to electronically collect their work over time, reflect upon their personal and academic growth, and then share selected items with others, such as professors, advisors, and potential employers." Doing philosophy with four-year-olds is interesting. As students from Rollins's P4C courses have come to apply for jobs, internships, and graduate school, a growing number of them have successfully used their P4C work as talking points.

CONCLUSION

In one respect, a college P4C course is simply an outgrowth of normal discussion-based pedagogy. We might think of a philosophy instructor's typical role as setting the parameters of discussion, establishing *how* students should interact and what they should talk *about*, leaving *what* to say to them. P4C merely invites children into the mix. The synergy between children and students is electric. In this shared community of inquiry, students and children are challenged to express new ideas and are motivated to stretch their minds as they engage in a joint endeavor.

One hard-to-measure outcome of the P4C project is what we might call its "fierce loyalty quotient." The great majority of students who go through this program come out ready to lead the revolution of pre-K12 education reform. Ten of them served as interns, test-driving draft lesson arcs from *Ethics for the Very Young* (Kenyon, Terorde-Doyle, and Carnahan 2019). A number have switched majors into philosophy, psychology, or early education. While the program is only a few years old, some of its initial wave of graduates are carrying on this work after college.

Alex Earl (religion '14) went on to complete a master of arts in religion at Yale and is now teaching at Pacifica, a Christian High School in Los Angeles. He is helping revise the school's liberal arts curriculum and teaches courses in political theory, twentieth-century thought, and a "church history" seminar whose two semesters are framed around Plato and Aristotle.

Mollie Jones (English and philosophy '15) is teaching at the Stony Brook School on Long Island. In 2017 she was hired to develop and coordinate a P4C summer program for the Briya Public Charter Schools in Washington, D.C. Her lessons have been used in bilingual classrooms across four campuses with children ages four to twelve.

Lexi Tomkunas (psychology and philosophy '18) has developed a P4C after-school program at Fern Creek Elementary, a Title I school in Orlando. In her psychology senior thesis, chaired by Sharon Carnahan, she developed an assessment tool for Rollins's approach to pre-K philosophy and organized four student interns to run lessons at Welbourne Day Nursery, a voluntary pre-K in Winter Park, Florida. She is spending the coming two years teaching in Miami through Teach for America, after which she plans to pursue a PhD in education policy and a career in the K12 policy sector.

Simon Says and mixing paint might seem like child's play. Yet students who can break down philosophical ideas and methods to their most basic components and then reassemble them for groups of four-year-olds tend to develop a critical eye for systems. Beyond philosophy, the P4C program has provided a springboard for students to pursue policy work in city planning, STEM education, and family healthcare administration. In short, the P4C program is producing the sort of nimble and engaged students a liberal education ought to produce. Schools would do well to take seriously the benefits of such programs for children and students alike.

NOTES

1. See chapter 5 in this anthology.
2. For clarity's sake, these two age groups will be referred to as "children" and "students."
3. This chapter has benefited from discussions with Susan Russinoff, who developed a similar course at Tufts University, spring 2018, working with children from kindergarten through second grade. Thanks also go to Mollie Jones, Sharon Carnahan, Diane Terorde-Doyle, and Nancy Chick for commenting on drafts of this chapter.

4. The present chapter is mostly prescriptive. A discussion of the process of developing Wartenberg's methods for use in pre-K is available (Kenyon and Terorde-Doyle 2017b). Gaut and Gaut provide an alternative approach to pre-K philosophy (2012).

5. The point is the discussion, not the art. Tufts students working with children from kindergarteners through second grade note that this use of art "was a great way to do the first few lessons, but then some of the groups of children seemed to tire of the same pattern" (Susan Russinoff, email to author, June 21, 2018). As with any scaffold, the art should be dispensed with when it no longer serves its purpose.

6. The Social Learning theory of Lev Vygotsky (1896–1934) better explains the non-egocentric behavior displayed by children in Rollins's P4C program. See Carol Garhart Mooney (2000).

7. Children sometimes attempt to "straddle" the sides of the river. If this will derail the discussion, do not allow it. Otherwise, see whether they can give a good reason for taking both sides.

8. This is taken from Kenyon, Terorde-Doyle, and Carnahan (2019).

9. The fall 2015 version of this course attempted a philosophy survey with pre-K children. The results were not great. The *number* of areas covered should be kept to a minimum; *which* areas is another question.

10. Each group spends three weeks on a given topic: courage, moderation, or friendship (Ancient); respect, rules, competing pleasures, or intent vs. consequences (Modern). Different groups may explore different topics. The sequence of Pragmatist sources, many of them from Rollins's own history, comes from a course co-taught with Lisa "Ryan" Musgrave.

11. This draws on principles of Backwards Course Design (Wiggins and McTighe 2005).

12. See also Sharon Carnahan (2019), who discusses P4C as one of several projects housed within Rollins's lab school. Her arguments about student learning, also drawing from AAC&U, may be readily transferred across disciplinary lines.

13. Susan Russinoff reports of her Tufts course, "One of my more gifted philosophy majors was paired with a young woman who had struggled to pass logic the previous semester. It turned out the female student has an extraordinary talent for communicating with young children and a natural ability for talking to kids about philosophy, while the 'more gifted' philosophy major was time after time frustrated by how difficult he found advancing the discussions with the kids. It was a really valuable experience for both of them. A wonderful dynamic" (email to author, June 21, 2018).

14. On one occasion, a student asked children to name a time they were brave, and a little girl replied, "Stairs!" The student concluded that four-year-olds are incapable of meaningful philosophical conversation. This same student later spoke with the girl's teachers and learned that the girl was afraid of heights and had been referring to a time that she overcame this fear by climbing a set of stairs. In this instance, the four-year-old understood the student perfectly. It was the student who had to learn to listen more seriously to the insights of others.

15. This approach to teaching writing is indebted to Cornell University's Knight Institute for Writing in the Disciplines (Monroe 2003).

REFERENCES

American Association of Colleges & Universities (AAC&U). "High-Impact Educational Practices." https://www.aacu.org/leap/hips. Accessed July 17, 2018.

Carnahan, Sharon. "The Role of the Laboratory School in a 21st Century Liberal Education." In *Contemporary Perspectives in Early Childhood Education*, edited by Olivia Saracho. Special edition, *Laboratory Schools* (2019).

Gaut, Berys, and Morag Gaut. *Philosophy for Young Children: A Practical Guide*. London: Routledge, 2012.

Kenyon, Erik, and Diane Terorde-Doyle. "The Three R's of Thinking: Nurturing Discussion in Preschools." *ASCD Express* 12, no. 10 (2017a). http://www.ascd.org/ascd-express/vol12/1210-kenyon.aspx.

Kenyon, Erik, and Diane Terorde-Doyle. "Art & Dialogue: An Experiment in Pre-K Philosophy." *Analytic Teaching and Philosophical Praxis* 7, no. 2 (2017b): 26–35. http://journal.viterbo.edu/index.php/atpp/article/view/1153.

Kenyon, Erik, Diane Terorde-Doyle, and Sharon Carnahan. *Ethics for the Very Young*. Lanham, MD: Rowman & Littlefield, 2019.

Kuh, George. *High-Impact Educational Practices: What They Are, Who Has Access to Them, and Why They Matter*. Washington, DC: Association of American Colleges and Universities, 2008.

Monroe, Jonathan, ed. *Local Knowledges, Local Practices: Writing in the Disciplines at Cornell*. Pittsburgh, PA: University of Pittsburgh Press, 2003.

Mooney, Carol Garhart. *Theories of Childhood: An Introduction to Dewey, Montessori, Erikson, Piaget & Vygotsky*. St. Paul, MN: Redleaf Press, 2000.

Wartenberg, Thomas. *Big Ideas for Little Kids*. Lanham, MD: Rowman & Littlefield, 2014.

Wiggins, Grant, and Jay McTighe. *Understanding by Design*. Alexandria, VA: Association for Supervision and Curriculum Development, 2005.

Chapter Two

Restoring Wonder

The Benefits and Challenges of Doing Philosophy in Mixed-Aged Groups

Stephen Kekoa Miller

> I believe it is very likely that men, if they ever should lose their ability to wonder and thus cease to ask unanswerable questions, also will lose the faculty of asking the answerable questions upon which every civilization is founded.
>
> —Hannah Arendt

Discovering the Philosophy for Children movement can completely alter the classroom practice of even the most experienced teacher. Years ago, Oakwood Friends School developed an extensive program in the history of philosophy. These courses were viewed as particularly challenging, and as a result, restricted to the oldest students. After observing sessions of very young children doing philosophy, however, this began to change.

It soon became clear that there was great virtue in extending the philosophy experience to younger students, both by opening up established electives to students in earlier grades and by designing a new ninth-grade class. The next year philosophy was taken into the middle school grades from sixth to eighth. In designing this course, high school student participation seemed to be an essential dimension. As a result, high school TAs have been involved in the middle school philosophy courses since their inception.

Inspired by the enthusiasm the courses generated, the school began to move the experience upward, hosting a series of Evening Philosophy sessions open to students, parents, faculty, and board members. In 2018, we saw a further expansion by adding a virtual element; using Google Hangouts, we were able to include graduates and board members who lived far away in a conversation covering more than a fifty-year span in ages.

This chapter will discuss the methods employed in these programs. The main question this chapter aims to address asks why a model of open philosophical inquiry, which doesn't aim to reach a specific endpoint, can have such a powerfully positive effect when conducted in a setting of mixed ages. In the end, this open philosophical inquiry can go at least partway toward undoing some of the negative consequences of current systematic denigration of children's voices.

THE AIMS OF A PHILOSOPHY PROGRAM

Philosophy programs and courses vary widely in curricula, methods, and approaches. It is important to differentiate between these different types and to link these with what they might be trying to accomplish. Ann Gazzard usefully distinguishes between three perspectives on philosophy itself:

> There is the understanding of philosophy as a type of striving associated with seeking to know how to live a better life suggested.... Secondly, there is a view which renders it a specific body of problems and/or the history of the ideas of past and present philosophers.... Thirdly and more recently, there is the view that philosophy is a particular way of thinking most often cast as reflective thinking. (1996, 9)

Put another way, these perspectives could divide into pragmatic effects on life choices, content mastery of a tradition, and finally a systematic method of thinking that can also be taught.

There are clearly virtues to all three approaches, and most philosophy programs will address all three at different points. A program that only teaches critical reasoning begins to look not much different from an SAT prep course, and any approach severed fully from the historical tradition of philosophy loses a chance to let students learn from the great conversations that have flowed over time.

This would be true even for philosophy programs with grade school students; for these cases, the names of famous philosophers may not be mentioned, but the manner in which they frame questions can invigorate even sessions involving picture books. Overemphasis on the first of these would be in danger of making it not a philosophy program at all, but more akin to career counseling.

Of course, the three perspectives described above only begin to describe the aims one might have for a philosophy program. For instance, a great deal of discussion has centered around whether or not a course of moral philosophy ought to aim to make students morally better people rather than simply better at moral reasoning or more knowledgeable about past answers to moral dilemmas.

Some recent work in moral psychology points to ways this type of moral improvement might be possible (Miller 2016). Other interesting aims might include using philosophical tools to illuminate and contest unconscious bias (Miller 2018) or using philosophical practice to intentionally engage in unlearning (Miller 2017).

Courses oriented around a particular time period, tradition, or topic in philosophy will by their nature have a very different objective than those that aim to bring the methods of critical reasoning outside of the classroom to help students behave and communicate more effectively in general. It will become clear that the use of a selective, targeted use of Community of Inquiry methodology will vary in relation to this question.

As an example, a class on epistemology (the theory of knowledge) may not aim to end with a final answer about which theory is true; however, it will, presumably, evaluate students on their ability to articulate clearly what Locke or Hume had to say about a particular issue. An open-inquiry session about the same topic may well not have any final answer in mind and the participants and leaders may well feel it a success if it ends in total perplexity (Miller 2017). By the end of the discussion, the views and/or names of prominent figures from the past may never have come up.

The programs described here will mostly involve philosophy sessions of the second type. However, even more traditional courses in the history of philosophy vein might well usefully employ these methods in sections of a class period as well, although any course that asks teachers to evaluate the students with a final grade will find open-inquiry classes more challenging in achieving this.

COMMUNITY OF INQUIRY

While it is not in the scope of this chapter to examine all of the nuances of Community of Inquiry methods, there are a few general points to be made. A Community of Inquiry by nature will always have a moderator. The literature about what this role should look like is full of heated and sometimes polemical debate about the method, need for training, and ultimate goal of this moderator.

What's important to remember here is that a powerful and effective Community of Inquiry can be multiply realized. Depending on the size of the group, age of the participants, level of philosophical background, and amount of practice from previous sessions, different techniques should be employed. Two key elements are necessary, however.

First is the importance of inspiring independent thought in the participants. Gilbert Ryle expressed it this way: "Now the notion of thinking is the notion of thinking for oneself, of making one's own try, however perfunctory and diffident, at some problem, task, or difficulty" (1979, 18). Thinking for oneself is not the same as thinking in a group, however.

The second essential aspect is the fact that in a group there will be disagreement. The process of expressing and evaluating these differences in a safe communal setting is the heart of the matter. By the end of a session, almost certainly, then, significant and mutually exclusive perspectives may remain live. Ending without resolution need not be deemed a failure.

A Community of Inquiry can begin with reference to one of several favorite procedural paradoxes, the first from an undergraduate mentor: "By the end of this session, we will not be any closer to a final discovery of truth, but we will be further from the beginning." Or: "In this session there will not be any right answers but we may find some wrong ones." While the beginning premise of a Community of Inquiry might initially appear to require a commitment to relativism, this is not necessarily the case.

In a fascinating discussion of epistemological issues arising from a Community of Inquiry, Maughn Rollins considers both *realists*, who need the critical element of a Community of Inquiry "as the only means by which the reasonableness of their truth can be fully appreciated" (1995, 32) and what he calls *first order non-realists*. The latter seek the multitude of perspectives of a Community of Inquiry since they suggest that "the goal of inquiry is to make one's understanding more and more comprehensive by learning to understand different points of view. In all areas of inquiry, that perspective is superior which subsumes the most points of view" (1995, 32).

Only those s*econd-order non-realists* who resist a synthesis of viewpoints then "must face the possibility of radical relativism" (1995, 37). Reaching a point at the end where disagreement remains and no final answers have been achieved not only needn't be seen as a failure, but importantly doesn't have to suggest that all answers are equally valid.

In the end, then, a Community of Inquiry isn't committed to a particular epistemology, but does need to begin with the premise of what Peirce and Dewey call "fallibilism." In this context, it can be seen as "a willingness to be corrected and an acknowledgment of possible error or perspectivalness" (Turgeon 2009, 48). A Community of Inquiry, then, is a method committed to bringing out multiple perspectives, critiquing them, and optimally causing all views to gain in precision and nuance through the process of the conversation.

DESCRIPTION OF OAKWOOD FRIENDS SCHOOL PROGRAMS

Outside of the more traditional history of philosophy courses it offers, Oakwood Friends School has instituted two new ways of bringing philosophy into the community. Initially, after finding out about the Philosophy for Children movement, the emphasis was on bringing younger students into philosophy courses by both instituting a ninth-grade critical thinking class and altering course requirements to allow younger students into preexisting courses.

These changes were both successful but stuck by the aims described previously as immersion into the tradition and instruction in reasoning. Most of the teaching that was done in these course involved a traditional Socratic-questioning-style method (Miller 2017). The newest offerings look to put the Community of Inquiry more at the heart of the program.

With this in mind, the first of these involved bringing philosophy into the middle school. The middle school philosophy program as originally envisaged met once weekly over the course of a trimester with one of the grades of the middle school at a time. The class met originally for forty-five minutes at a time, and the students were not graded. Over time, due to scheduling considerations and the uneven distribution of numbers in the three middle school grades, we moved to once a week, sixty minutes, and with mixed grade levels.

After the first year, inspired by other programs including the Mount Holyoke course pioneering the use of college student philosophy moderators (Wartenberg 2003), high school teaching assistants (TAs) entered the picture. Currently, each trimester upper-grade high school students who have been successful in philosophy classes may serve as TAs.

Over the past few years, that has meant one or two TAs serving at a time. In this capacity, they help guide the conversation, plan out one or two philosophy sessions toward the end of the term, and, importantly, participate in all of the discussions and activities. Bringing in the TAs immediately and significantly deepened the middle school philosophy program, despite some challenges, described below.

The second new program over the past few years has been dubbed Evening Philosophy. Largely inspired by student interest, approximately bimonthly a group of students, faculty, parents, and board members began to meet in the evenings to convene a Community of Inquiry. Over the past few years, topics have included philosophy of education, epistemology, banality of evil, free will, personal identity and social categories, philosophy of language, happiness, and virtue ethics, among others.

The topic for the next session is generally agreed upon in a very general way at the end of a session. In the weeks leading up to a new discussion, a document of readings from the philosophical tradition, popular culture, and newer sources is shared with all potential attendees. While the readings for most sessions are curated by the moderator, the most successful evenings have been ones when a number of participants have also found readings to share. The readings are optional but sessions where a number of participants have done the reading tend to be the most productive.

In the last year, an interesting new development has involved using technology to allow virtual attendees. This allows former students and board members to join the discussion as a projected image on a screen. The technology is set up to allow for someone who has begun to speak to immediately take the focal spot in the center of the screen.

The best part of this (aside from the inherent excitement of having a discussion with participants ranging from Europe to California) has been the fact that each of these sessions has happened to fall into a highly varied mix of graduates and former teachers and board members. Importantly, these sessions often have an age range of more than fifty years.

These two new programs have not been without challenges. I'll first share some responses to a survey that prompted participants (students, faculty, board members, and TAs) to reflect on what hadn't worked well about mixed-age Community of Inquiry in the middle school. Here are a few from different constituencies:

Two middle schoolers describe one challenge effectively:

- *Parker, seventh grade*: "Sometimes the older kids felt superior so they would just say that they were right."
- *Hannah, eighth grade*: "In middle school philosophy some people are immature and do not take things as seriously."
- *Ted, music faculty*: "Occasionally there will be one or two individuals who talk constantly and monopolize the discussion. These loquacious participants can come from any age-group, but, at least in my experience, they tend to be younger people with less experience discussing ideas in a group."
- *James, board of managers*: "At times, the questions posed for discussion can get lost when they touch on or lie close by issues of immediate concern or preoccupation for the younger people [students]. This can be [has been, in my experience] corrected by facilitators, or even by other participants."

To generalize, some of the biggest challenges facing mixed-age Community of Inquiry philosophy sessions over the past few years have centered around a few distinct points. With middle school into early high school aged students, there is an enormous difference in maturity levels both between and within grades. Finding a balance between open inquiry and a teacher-centered discussion can be challenging, especially with TAs in their first few attempts. The times when it has been necessary for the teacher to intercede and take control of the discussion has had the effect of deflating the feeling of open discourse and undermining the authority of the TA.

This touches directly on two points of some contention among practitioners of Community of Inquiry methods: whether or not it's ever okay to use moderators without specific professional licensure and whether or not it's an abuse of power for a moderator to choose the questions for discussion or to interrupt a discussion that's going off the rails to get it back on track. The second point will be addressed below.

While the first of these, the use of untrained moderators, is a real concern, our program has aimed to address this by having both the class and the TA train together for weeks before the first time a high school student TA will moderate. In the cases the teacher has had to intervene and help regain control, both the students and the TA professed to having learned a lot from the experience.

Another area of difficulty in the middle school philosophy program involves the fact that TAs don't come to the project with teaching experience. The sessions they plan often involve too much lecture or misunderstand the timing of discussion topics (although some of the best discussions have somehow emerged from a tremendously awkward start—the students seem to will the TA to succeed).

A final point with middle school ages involves topics. While social and ethical issues are of paramount concern for students at this age, they also bring up the most difficult discussion dynamics. Sometimes beginning a term with more abstract metaphysical and epistemological topics can help form a Community of Inquiry more effectively at the start.

Once the communal norms are in place, social and ethical topics are more easily handled. At their best, however, middle school students still often find it challenging to escape the details of their daily social turmoil with their peers. Even this overly anecdotal orientation they may take toward social and ethical issues may still be useful; anecdote can here be understood as "a unit of self-narrative . . . a principal way to offer a new philosophy of the self" (Laverty 2003, 32).

Ultimately, running a Community of Inquiry with middle grade students seems to run more of a risk of sudden eruption of emotion than either younger students (often very well trained at taking turns) or older students (more tempered in their emotional expression), but this doesn't negate the value of the endeavor. In general, if middle grade students have a harder time staying on task and hearing their peers respectfully than both younger and older students, then the challenge becomes finding a balance between the open discourse and the more teacher-directed lesson. The use of teacher authority to achieve this will be discussed in a later section.

The work to achieve a working Community of Inquiry is worth these challenges, however. I experience almost daily anecdotal confirmation of how powerful a Community of Inquiry can be. What has been particularly interesting has been how overtly the participants' experience has been informed and improved by having a mix of ages present. Nearly everyone taking the survey saw this as being a central part of the experience. Here is a sampling from a number of different participants:

The emphasis of these comments focused on the differing perspectives and styles various ages bring:

- *Parker, seventh grade:* "We could all talk about things that if we all had just one age group we might not have the same in-depth conversations."
- *Lily, current TA:* "As a sophomore it was inspiring to see seniors and juniors really participate full heartedly in conversations. Now taking philosophy with middle schoolers I can see they are so much more unapologetic and excited to share their opinions than what I have grown accustomed to with high schoolers, and is invigorating as it was to be introduced to the Oakwood learning environment for the first time."
- *Ted, music faculty:* "Also, the fact that the issues we discuss are important to people in different age groups makes the sessions feel more meaningful and powerful to me than if the topics seemed pertinent only to a small group of people."
- *Hannah, eighth grade:* "The younger people seemed to give more practical answers."

What these responses have in common is the experience of nearly everyone at mixed-aged sessions, that something special and uncommon happens when people from different ages get together to do philosophy. The next sections will discuss some conceptual matters involving the philosophy of childhood and why a Community of Inquiry model is particularly adept at addressing some fundamental questions related to hermeneutics and age.

An interesting first question here is about what effect this process has on its participants. One way of looking at this is that after spending an hour or more working hard at a question that nearly everyone will agree is important to them all, at the end, this question remains unanswered. This can be frustrating. The first time reading one of Plato's early dialogues such as *Lysis* or *Phaedrus* or *Euthyphro* as an undergraduate can leave a reader wanting to shout at Socrates, "So then, what IS friendship? What IS love? What IS piety?" Fascinatingly, Community of Inquiry sessions don't generally end this way, despite not providing final answers.

Something happens in a community of sincere people engaging and thinking together that is experienced as productive despite it not reaching these answers. Of course, Socrates's interlocutors would not have felt this because he never gives them a chance for a true dialogue; for him, the process is rigged. Thinking *together*, though, seems to cause quite a different emotional response in participants. Here is a final sample of responses of how different constituencies experienced this aporetic ending:

- *Alexandria, former TA:* "When you are in math or history courses, you are introduced to a solid fact, "this is how it happened" or "this equals this." However, in a philosophy course you fathom the world of possibility, trying to intellectualize and come to the conclusion of no conclusion. It exercises the brain in a completely different light and way."
- *Lily, former TA:* "It is brilliant! . . . There is a perfect balance between the possibilities that open with no right or wrong answer and no endpoint, and the structure of studying and becoming familiar with the ideas that are already out there."
- *Parker, seventh grade:* "It was kind of nice to be able to have a discussion with no answer that kept branching off into different things. . . . It had less tension *so I felt safer sharing*." (emphasis added)
- *Bianca, eighth grade:* "It's interesting because of the amount of times an opinion can change. Also, *since there is no end point, no one gets angry about their opinion being right*. It's all about listening, thinking, and bouncing ideas off each other." (emphasis added)
- *Michael, humanities faculty:* "I like how the discussion tends to erase the student/teacher, adult/child boundary. We're all simply minds using language to engage and connect, and there's something essentially human about it. Insight has no use for these boundaries, but there aren't many situations where one can interact in this manner. Being forced to think isn't always comfortable."
- *James, board of managers:* "In matters of philosophy I don't believe there are 'right' answers, only good questions. In which case, there can be no end point, only ongoing exploration. The Evening Philosophy Program provides both in an inclusive community of inquiry."

EPISTEMIC INJUSTICE AND CHILDHOOD

These insights, and much anecdotal experience, lead one to wonder why so many people, especially children, find the experience of an open-ended Community of Inquiry so powerful. Some recent work linking Miranda Fricker's notion of epistemic injustice to childhood helps to explain this to some degree. Then, when exploring a theory of childhood, we can see why it's so important.

Fricker's book *Epistemic Injustice* does a lovely job explaining what it looks like to be denied agency as a knower, and also tells a strong story about the consequences. She states that "No wonder, then, that being insulted, undermined, or otherwise wronged in one's capacity as a giver of knowledge is something that can cut deep. No wonder too that in contexts of oppression the powerful will be sure to undermine the powerless in just that capacity, for it provides a direct route to undermining them in their very humanity (2009, 44).

Whether or not school systems are designed to enact just that process on schoolchildren needn't be decided here. It is indisputable that the effect of most modern systems of education is just this, however.

Fricker's framework is promising for understanding issues of age-based epistemic injustice. The connection of epistemic injustice to young people is an important one; it is not unproblematic however, because there are times and situations where almost everyone would agree that young people should not be deemed epistemically equal.

School is in particular a good example of this; most students will never feel epistemically equal to their teachers in a math class, but they usually won't feel oppressed by this fact. In regards to the mastery of information and skills, younger students, by their very developmental age, are usually unable to serve as equal owners of knowledge (some useful exceptions allow students to share their knowledge with each other, but rarely on equal footing with teachers).

While this may be true, students are often denied agency in areas where their voices can be or should be taken equally. Students can identify the salience of information, can articulate how the skill acquisition they're aiming for can fit into different views of what a good life looks like, and can be fully equal participants in the kinds of "unanswerable" questions that philosophy has always prized. In fact, we might think that the more "philosophical" a question is, the more likely children are to come up with brilliant, counterintuitive, and creative perspectives than those more familiar with "how things are" are likely to arrive at.

The form of testimonial injustice, termed by Fricker as identity power, involves discounting a child's testimony even when the situation at hand concerns the child's own experiences. It's easy to see how this could extend to discounting a child's pain, anxiety, excitement, hopes, and many, many other forms of direct subjective experience. Fricker describes this experience like this:

> When you find yourself in a situation in which you seem to be the only one to feel the dissonance between received understanding and your own intimated

sense of a given experience, it tends to knock your faith in your own ability to make sense of the world (2009, 163).

Many children, over years of unintentional reinforcement, stop expecting to be taken seriously. This is painful, but to have this happen during the years when one's sense of self is being developed, it becomes devastating.

The end result is that for far too many young students, by the time they are reaching the middle grades, they have stopped thinking of themselves as potential creators of knowledge, have stopped valuing their interpretations of the salience of what they're learning and finally become alienated and disaffected in such a way that they evade thinking about the most important questions of all. Empirical studies bear this out.

In "The Illusion of Incompetence among Academically Competent Children," Deborah Phillips shows how "learned helplessness" and the "loss of persistence" are the final result of this process (1984, 2011). This grim picture has a long history as well: "Plato often associates children with slaves, women and animals, and both he and Aristotle group children with the "sick, the drunk, the insane and the wicked" (Kennedy 2006, 9).

One of the biggest contributors to epistemic injustice in regards to children seems to come directly out of a poor understanding of who children are—so that even when their competence and sincerity are recognized, they are denied the ability to be subjects of knowledge since they are deemed sincere and competent *for children*.

However, being treated with epistemic justice in a Community of Inquiry can at least partially explain how exhilarating children find doing philosophy. Which precise understanding of childhood we adopt will strongly affect the stance we end up taking toward actual children we encounter and as a result set the tone for how their testimony is received.

PHILOSOPHY OF THE CHILD

Gareth Matthews's *The Philosophy of Childhood* first raised some of the key questions about how children should be understood. In this text, he critiques two models of childhood: the developmental and the recapitulation theory. While it is clear that children do indeed develop, the essential question involves whether or not rationality and philosophical thinking is maturational.

Matthews offers highly compelling arguments suggesting that while children do change and improve at some things, they also are able to follow and present arguments fully well, and are not, as Jung famously described, "prerational . . . and pre-scientific" (1994, 27). The developmental model would have us see children as on an arc toward a mature perspective, a journey almost all of us make. As a result, children's perspectives would always be merely provisional, immature, and only to be taken seriously as a marker of progress toward a more correct, mature perspective.

A related, and likewise flawed, view, the recapitulation theory, sees children as going through stages while they develop that mirror those of the species as a whole. This view has the problem stated above while also suggesting that human thought as a whole has gotten more mature—that Plato's thought is less mature than Wittgenstein. This implies a double injustice, both to age and to human society over time.

Ultimately, Matthews concludes that children may well be better than adults at a few essential parts of traditional philosophical practice. Firstly, "Children in their simple directness often bring us adults back to basics" (1994, 67). Secondly, moral imagination: "People become overwhelmed by the problems of the society around them, or increasingly preoccupied by their personal agendas. . . . A child's naive question can awaken our sleeping imagination and sympathy, and even move us towards moral action" (1994, 65).

Given that all of us eventually suffer from what Freud termed *childhood amnesia*, if children have these important insights, we can't rely on our own memories of traversing that forgotten territory. We need current residents to share these. David Kennedy describes school as "an institution of subjection," the place where we become subjects (2006, 153).

Since in children the process is not yet complete, it becomes especially essential for adults to encounter children to be reminded of alternative ways of being and seeing. Despite often patronizing views of children's philosophizing as cute or charming, these ways of opening up the subjunctive may indeed be essential for adult well-being as well; this starts to point the way to why mixed-age groupings can be so powerful for both school-aged and older participants.

In addition to the question of how children as potential subjects of knowledge are understood, social inequalities based on age will always affect this issue. Teachers are endowed with structural means of power that can strongly affect the lives of their students, and in a philosophical discussion can serve as a battering ram in tearing down children's alternative perspectives. The question of whether or not this inequality must prevent teachers and students from sharing insights effectively then becomes important. While teachers' institutional power is very often abused, fortunately, it is not inevitably disabling of epistemic justice.

THE EXERCISE OF TEACHER AUTHORITY

Given that teachers in school and even moderators in a Community of Inquiry carry with them institutional authority, it is worth thinking about whether or not these structural imbalances would cancel out the potential of a mixed-age philosophy group to engender open philosophical thinking. Thomas Wartenberg, in his 1990 book *The Forms of Power: From Domination to Transformation*, introduces an essential corrective to earlier understandings of power.

Taking account of the social structures that lead to hermeneutic injustice, we can also see clear to understanding how this same authority could be used in ways that would reduce epistemic injustice. In the book, Wartenberg contests "the assumption that power is dyadic . . . consisting of a dominant agent and a subordinate agent over whom he wields power" (1990, 141).

In this case, then, we'd need to consider that if the authority is socially situated, then the solution wouldn't simply entail an empathetic or kindly teacher. If the philosophical discussion is going to benefit the students, the very social institutional power here would need to be used to undo the hermeneutical injustice—it needs to be structural or programmatic. Wartenberg terms the *transformational* use of power as a wielding of authority in a way that could be deemed "positive" to benefit the agent over whom they are exercised (1990, 183).

A Community of Inquiry, in the way described previously, would be unlikely to involve grading (although Wartenberg shows how even grading can be accomplished in a transformational manner). However, it would still use the socially situated power of the teacher to force students into following discussion norms, speaking in a particular manner and style and listening respectfully. Once this is accomplished, however, the transformation that can be exacted would mean that "the teacher here is not one person; the children (teachers?) are listening responsively to each other and construct new thoughts together" (Murris 2013, 205).

This suggests that there could be transformational use of power that would avoid a reliance on a developmental view of childhood, of assuming that the teacher knows the answers and the pupils' early attempts are merely provisional. The optimal situation here would involve reciprocal or "mutual transformation" (Kennedy 2006, 22). Finally, then, if it is the case that we are different people at different ages, a final question here concerns what children are best suited to teach.

SOCRATES, THE SUBJUNCTIVE, AND THE RESTORATION OF EPISTEMIC JUSTICE

While this discussion has focused on children, equally interesting things can be said about other age categories. Older people often are treated with epistemic injustice. In a sense, they're read through an inverted lens of the development theory; in this case rather than progressing toward an apex of human maturity, they're seen as declining away from it. As a result, even if they're seen as sincere, they're likely to be treated as not competent.

In Plato's *Republic*, Socrates opens up the discussion with an older character, Cephalus, in such a way that initially looks breathtaking in its rudeness. Socrates, in approaching the much older man, says this:

> I certainly will, Cephalus. In fact, I enjoy engaging in discussion with the very old. I think we should learn from them—since they are like people who have traveled a road that we too will probably have to follow—what the road is like, whether rough and difficult or smooth and easy. And I would be particularly glad to find out from you what you think about it, since you have reached the point in life the poets call old age's threshold. Is it a difficult time of life? What have you to report about it? (Plato and Reeve 2004, 2)

While it is undeniably indelicate to inquire about feelings about death from the elderly, Socrates asks the question from a position prompting epistemic justice: He takes the testimony and interpretation of Cephalus seriously. In fact, taking the testimony of others seriously can often cause discomfort. Socratic *aporia* is premised on the fact that this discomfort can be useful (Miller 2017).

However, it isn't *always* useful to have one's perspective questioned. Without the proper staging to convert the school setting to one of transformational power, Socratic-style questioning can lead to deflation and discouragement when the goal is, after all, open philosophical thinking in a context of hermeneutic justice. A mixed-age group of people engaged in philosophical questioning stand the danger of having the older participants discount or patronize the younger ones, denying them their testimony.

Younger participants have at times suggested older ones were out of touch. A successful Community of Inquiry will allow the transformation of the whole group; through collectively submitting to rules of discourse, it becomes possible for everyone to benefit, even if the rules and structures themselves have arrived from power exercised by the moderator/teacher.

So, what is it that allows children to feel equal as subjects of knowledge inside and outside of a classroom? It seems clear that the skill younger children come to the table most equipped to offer is perhaps the most important: the ability to think counterfactually. While this skill may not be useful in all fields (speculation about what would have happened if a particular historical event had played out differently or what it would imply if a math question had a different answer is rarely stimulating), in philosophy, it is at the heart of the matter.

The ability to think "as-if" allows us the ability to get beyond the given; all real philosophical thinking attaches to this instinct, and it is really here where children can best teach us all. A well-run Community of Inquiry would be one where these skills are valued and encouraged. Children notice appreciably when a moderator says with wonder, "I've never thought about this question like that before," and means it as a compliment.

Kwame Anthony Appiah's 2018 book, *As-If: Idealization and Ideals*, terms this process of suspension of the "real" as idealization (following Vaihinger). Appiah sees this as creating the opportunity for multiple perspectives. The best opportunity to have a subject matter engage these multiple perspectives is often in the Community of Inquiry setting, especially a diverse one, and most especially in an age-diverse one.

This is true when it comes to receiving the valuable insights of students; students tend not to have the same access to presses, public space and/or the sincere and open ears of adults. Therefore, any opportunity that their voices can be raised then becomes quite especially meaningful for them.

To have their insights not only held as equally worth exploring (and critiquing!) as the moderator's but as Aristotle's as well goes a long way toward inspiring students to attempt to be subjects of knowledge in other areas. It is very common to hear from other teachers about how middle school and other evening philosophy discussions bleed into other subjects (including home dinner tables, sometimes to parents' chagrin), with the students confidently leading the conversation. If Appiah is correct then,

> Once we come to see that many of our best theories are idealizations, we will also see why our best chance of understanding the world must be to have a plurality of ways of thinking about it. This book is about why we need a multitude of pictures of the world. It is a gentle jeremiad against theoretical monism (2018, x).

The natural skill many children have at the subjunctive comes from this same vein; in sharing this skill, they often help older participants realize that views they assume are natural or obvious are very much open for questioning. Older participants can often offer powerful discussions of their experiences, sometimes showing how perspectives that might seem flawed are adopted for good reason.

A Community of Inquiry will demand that each view be defended and nuanced as the conversation goes forward. There is no single magic bullet that can restore epistemic justice for either children, the elderly, or any other group that suffers from having its testimony treated as unworthy of taking seriously. However, mixed-age philosophy sessions can offer restorative experiences when children and adults can come alive with the joy of thinking in a group. The students who have experienced this now look for more and more of these moments. As their talent at idealization causes their teachers to question previously unquestioned classroom practices, everyone can only benefit.

CONCLUSION

These initiatives alone are not enough to disrupt the epistemic injustice suffered by the very young and very old. However this manner of engaging participants restores to those who have been harmed the desire and capacity to engage in dialogue with others whom they trust. The newly developed philosophy program at the Oakwood Friends School can thus be a model for the one way of doing philosophy in a setting that brings younger students and adults together and as a result, benefits them both.

REFERENCES

Bingham, Charles. *Authority Is Relational: Rethinking Educational Empowerment.* Albany, NY: State University of New York Press, 2009.

Brenifer, Oscar. "How to Avoid Children's Questions." *Thinking: The Journal of Philosophy for Children* 16, no. 4 (2003): 29–32. doi:10.5840/thinking200316413.

Burroughs, Michael D., and Deborah Tollefsen. "Learning To Listen: Epistemic Injustice and the Child." *Episteme* 13, no. 03 (01, 2016): 359–77. doi:10.1017/epi.2015.64.

Douthat, Ross. "Power to the Parents." *New York Times.* March 3, 2018. https://www.nytimes.com/2018/03/03/opinion/sunday/parents-teenagers-voting.html.

Gazzard, Ann. "Philosophy for Children and the Discipline of Philosophy." *Thinking: The Journal of Philosophy for Children* 12, no. 4 (1996): 9–16. doi:10.5840/thinking19961243.

Gosnell, Nelda, and Henry Frankel. "Can We Help Children Think?" *Thinking: The Journal of Philosophy for Children* 1, no. 3 (1979): 74–76. doi:10.5840/thinking19791318.

Karaba, Robert. "Reconceptualizing the Aims in Philosophy for Children." *Thinking: The Journal of Philosophy for Children* 20, no. 1 (2012): 50–54. doi:10.5840/thinking2012201/27.

Kennedy, David. *The Well of Being: Childhood and Postmodern Subjectivity.* New York: Peter Lang, 2004.

Kyle, Judy A. "Managing Philosophical Discussions." *Thinking: The Journal of Philosophy for Children* 5, no. 2 (1984): 19–22. doi:10.5840/thinking19845217.

Laverty, Megan. "The Role of Confession in Community of Inquiry." *Thinking: The Journal of Philosophy for Children* 16, no. 3 (2003): 30–35. doi:10.5840/thinking20031636.

Matthews, Gareth B. *The Philosophy of Childhood.* Cambridge, MA: Harvard University Press, 1996.

Matthews, Gareth B. *Socratic Perplexity and the Nature of Philosophy.* Oxford: Oxford University Press, 1999.

McCall, Catherine C. *Transforming Thinking: Philosophical Inquiry in the Primary and Secondary Classroom.* London: Routledge, 2016.

Miller, Stephen Kekoa. "Socratic Aporia in the Classroom and the Development of Resilience." *Analytic Teaching and Philosophical Praxis* 38, no. 1 (2017). http://journal.viterbo.edu/index.php/atpp/article/view/1002.

Miller, Stephen Kekoa. "Your Feelings Are Wrong." *Analytic Teaching and Philosophical Praxis* 37, no. 1 (2016). http://journal.viterbo.edu/index.php/atpp/article/view/1147.

Murris, Karin. "The Epistemic Challenge of Hearing Child's Voice." *Studies in Philosophy and Education* 32, no. 3 (2013): 245–59. doi:10.1007/s11217-012-9349-9.

Phillips, Christopher. *Socrates Café: A Fresh Taste of Philosophy*. Cambridge, UK: Lutterworth, 2003.

Phillips, Deborah. "The Illusion of Incompetence among Academically Competent Children." *Child Development* 55, no. 6 (December 1984): 2000–2016. doi:10.2307/1129775.

Plato and C. D. C. Reeve. *Republic*. Indianapolis, IN: Hackett, 2004.

Rollins, Maughn. "Epistemological Considerations for the Community of Inquiry." *Thinking: The Journal of Philosophy for Children* 12, no. 2 (1995): 31–40. doi:10.5840/thinking199512220.

Ryle, Gilbert. "Thinking and Self-Teaching." *Thinking: The Journal of Philosophy for Children* 1, no. 3 (1979): 18–23. doi:10.5840/thinking1979134.

Turgeon, Wendy. "Transforming Thinking: Philosophical Inquiry in the Primary and Secondary Classroom." *Thinking: The Journal of Philosophy for Children* 19, no. 4 (2009): 46–48. doi:10.5840/thinking200919429.

Wartenberg, Thomas E. *The Forms of Power: From Domination to Transformation*. Philadelphia, PA: Temple University Press, 1990.

Wartenberg, Thomas E. "Teaching Philosophy by Teaching Philosophy Teaching." *Teaching Philosophy* 26, no. 3 (2003): 283–97. doi:10.5840/teachphil200326327.

Wartenberg, Thomas E. *Big Ideas for Little Kids: Teaching Philosophy through Children's Literature*. Lanham, MD: Rowman & Littlefield, 2014.

Chapter Three

Peace Building from Mali to Michigan

Stephen L. Esquith

> Education is almost as decisive as exposure to violence in inclining Malians to disavow the legitimacy of military rule.
>
> —Michael Bratton, founder and former executive director, *Afrobarometer*

In the struggle for democracy in Mali, education can be part of the solution, but it won't come easy. Prior to the 2012 coup d'état, there was a strong positive relationship between education and a wide range of measures of political engagement, both for students and their parents (Bleck 2015). Unfortunately, as Michael Bratton points out, when there are "low levels of education" for the majority of the population, this can be a "severe drag" on any attempt to protect human rights and sustain democratic development (2016, 452).

This has been the case in Mali since 2012. The coup did not result in the immediate loss of large numbers of lives compared to similar incidents elsewhere, however the continuing impact on Malians has been significant, including the impact on education and consequently on political legitimacy (Coulibaly and Coulibaly 2018).

While elementary and secondary school attendance has risen recently in some parts of the country, in northern and central regions public schools have been closed because of the direct threat of violence against teachers from insurgents and extremists. Higher education faces its own difficult challenges. Faculty salaries and facilities have stagnated while enrollments have swelled, and the result has been lengthy faculty and student strikes and protests.

Since 2014 the Ciwara School in Kati, Mali, and several related nongovernmental organizations have been the site of the peace-education program. This program is modeled on the kind of critical thinking and student-centered learning that Tom Wartenberg champions in *Big Ideas for Little Kids* (2014). The program extends the *Big Ideas* model of philosophy for children in two ways.

First, the teachers have created four new picture books for students in grades one through nine and extended the picture-book format in *Big Ideas* through a political simulation, the Mali Peace Game. Together, the books and the peace game have served as the basis for a performance-based pedagogy and local community dialogues.

Second, the program has created picture books and simulations for middle school and high school students in Lansing, Michigan, using the same pedagogical approach but with different content.[1] This chapter focuses on two of the four picture books developed at the Ciwara School which serve as the foundation for the other parts of the project in Mali and their Michigan counterparts. Each of the picture books addresses a different concept in global ethics and political philosophy central to democracy: human rights, care, responsibility, and justice.

PEACEKEEPING AND PEACE BUILDING

The challenge facing peacekeepers, even in the best of circumstances, is what one former diplomat has called "the fog of peace" (Guéhenno 2015). Peacekeepers, whether they are designing humanitarian aid or securing a highway against terrorist explosive devices, must make difficult moral decisions under conditions of great uncertainty. Knowing whom to trust in high-level negotiations, at a traffic stop, or at the entrance to a refugee camp requires moral judgment under extraordinary pressure (Levine 2014).

Peace builders recognize that ceasefires need to be declared, treaties need to be signed and honored, and the peacekeeping forces that assist in these measures are a necessary condition for peace building. However, they also recognize that peacekeeping, the way it has been done by even the most well-meaning and well-trained forces, is insufficient and can sometimes make conflicts more, not less, violent. The everyday routines, intellectual training, and social relationships among peacekeepers can handicap peacekeeping efforts and undermine peace building.

Peacekeepers often do not see the world the same way that the people whom they are there to assist do. Problems are compartmentalized even though they actually are interconnected. Peacekeepers rely on thematic professional knowledge that is often not context-dependent rather than on local knowledge, which is.

Local staff assisting peacekeepers have a more nuanced understanding of local norms and values but remain in subordinate positions, while the peacekeepers themselves often are cloistered and unfamiliar with the cultural norms of the people they are there to help (Autesserre 2014). To avoid these biases and traps, effective peacekeepers and especially more long-term peace builders must spend more time alongside their local partners, using local languages to better understand local conditions.

Peace building, in contrast to peacekeeping, aims at neither the complete cessation of violent hostilities nor the resolution of conflicts once and for all. Peace building assumes that conflicts will persist; its goal is to reduce the likelihood of violence and to create alternative ways of mediating conflict through dialogue and local political and cultural institutions and practices. Peace building is how democracy can emerge from the ruins.[2]

The peace-education work in Mali at the Ciwara School since 2012–2013 aspires to build peace locally in this democratic sense. It is based on a partnership with local teachers and artists. It is multilingual and integrates local cultural norms and practices into its projects. It is designed for the "long haul."[3]

In summer 2014 Michigan State University students and their faculty in the Residential College in the Arts and Humanities (RCAH) traveled back to Kati in response to the coup d'état and occupation of 2012–2013. MSU had been sending students and faculty to Mali for ten years prior to the coup to work with several small Malian nongovernmental organizations on community development projects. However, the heightened violence triggered by the coup demanded that attention be focused exclusively on peace building and democratic political education.

The team's goal in 2014 was to create a peace-education program using the tools of philosophy for children and the methods of local peace building developed by the international nongovernmental organization Interpeace. This task was approached through a collaboration with one of RCAH's partners in Mali, the Ciwara School, its parent Malian NGO, l'Institut pour l'Education Populaire (IEP), and most recently students and faculty from the Université des Lettres and des Science Humaine de Bamako.

THE CIWARA PICTURE BOOKS

The four picture books created by the program now are being used with approximately 350 students in grades one to nine at the Ciwara School and several neighboring schools in Kati, Mali. These books were composed with the help of the Language and Media Center of RCAH and small grants through

Michigan State University's Crowdpower website and the Public Affairs Office of the United States Embassy in Mali. Ciwara teachers, in consultation with RCAH faculty and students, wrote and illustrated these books in French, English, and Bamanankan, the most commonly spoken local native language in this part of Mali.

The books use traditional Malian fabric art familiar to the teachers and students to illustrate stories about the social conflicts and violent threats to security present in the everyday lives of Ciwara students and teachers. The use of fabric art for the picture books derives from several aspects of Malian culture. Using these colorful fabrics to illustrate a story is similar to telling the story in a traditional language. It affirms the value of the local culture and speaks to the students in a visual vocabulary (for example, *bogolan*, the traditional dyed fabric) that they recognize (Rovine 2008).

Before composing the picture books, the Malian teachers and students worked with RCAH faculty and students to create their own large *bogolan* banners that addressed the ongoing conflicts in Mali in 2014–2015. They did this under the tutelage of the well-known Malian art collective Groupe Kasobane, which taught them how to make *bogolan* and exploit its cultural resonance in Mali to make arguments of their own about war and peace.[4]

Then the teachers and students began to use commercial printed fabrics (commonly referred to as "African wax prints" used for clothing throughout West Africa) to create characters and landscapes in their new stories. They cut out small pieces of these colorful fabrics, some of which contained *bogolan* symbols or abstract versions of them, in order to "paint" the images they had sketched for their stories. The pages—text on one side and image on the other—were photographed and then professionally reprinted on durable paper.

All four of the printed Ciwara picture books address peace building in a discursive way; that is, they avoid positing universal moral values or drawing a single moral lesson from each story. Instead, they present conflicts through open-ended stories that highlight different realistic moral dilemmas and political conflicts the students can understand and discuss together.

They also introduce ways in which political dialogue may help to transform violent and potentially violent conflicts into opportunities for care, reconciliation, and justice. The basic idea is to help students recognize the uncritical assumptions they may be making in order to transform these conflicts into a peace-building process leading to more informed democratic participation (Richmond and Mitchell 2012).

This connection between the picture books and democratic political education is integral to philosophy for children. As Tom Wartenberg argues in *Big Ideas for Little Kids*, philosophy is a "game of moves," and teaching children the rules of the game prepares them for more than just philosophical discussion (2014, 37). These activities included the performance of short skits, the creation of new comic art, and the participation in political simulations and community dialogue forums.

The Ciwara teachers created their own detailed guide for teachers and learners for each of the four completed picture books. The guide for the first book, *The Challenge*, became the model for the guides for the other three books as well as a guide for the political simulation, the Mali Peace Game. The picture books have become the anchor for a Philosophy for Children program in which the "moves" the students learn through the books then guide their behavior and attitudes toward one another in these other activities, including actual community dialogues.

PHILOSOPHY FOR CHILDREN

The idea for using the Mali picture books as the basis for an approach to peace education originated in an earlier community civic engagement project in East Lansing, Michigan. RCAH students who had enrolled in one section of a required course in civic engagement read *Big Ideas for Little Kids* and used this as their text for a Philosophy for Children project in two fourth-grade classrooms in an elementary school with students from a mixture of socioeconomic classes.

The picture books they used were some of the ones in *Big Ideas* that deal with ethics and politics, including:

- *Frog and Toad Together* by Arnold Lobel;
- *Frederick* by Leo Lionni; and
- *The Giving Tree* by Shel Silverstein.

Using these picture books and dramatizations of them that the RCAH students created, the elementary school students learned how to think more philosophically. Their intuitions and curiosity were already well-aligned with some basic tenets of philosophical reflection and analysis. It was not a struggle to encourage them to give reasons for the positions they took, to listen to other points of view rather than reject them prematurely, and to use concrete examples and counterexamples to make and criticize arguments. They were, in Wartenberg's language, natural-born philosophers.

Having had this positive experience in East Lansing, it was decided to recruit some of the RCAH students to participate in the study-abroad program at the Ciwara School that had been taking place since 2004. In summer 2014, a new peace-education program was initiated. The first task was to teach the Ciwara teachers what it means to use picture books in a learner-centered philosophy classroom. This was not easy.

The traditional model of instruction in Mali institutionalized by the French in the twentieth century has long been teacher-centered: copy, memorize, and repeat. The Ciwara School has struggled against this French colonial model in form and content, but each year when they hire new teachers (because they cannot afford to pay as much as the larger public schools and their best teachers move on in a year or two), they have to train the new teachers to give up the colonial model.

Teacher training has turned out to be an ongoing challenge for the peace-education program. The first cohort of Ciwara teachers in the peace-education program in 2014 participated in an intensive six-week summer immersion with other Malians students from the teacher training college in Bamako, l'Ecole Normale Superieure (ENSUP).

Together with the RCAH study-abroad students, the three groups first read several of the Wartenberg picture books in very rough French and Bamanakan translations. Then, they were introduced to a few more books with similar themes, including Toni Morrison's *The Big Box* and a second book by Leo Lionni, *Swimmy*, again using translations made specifically for these discussions.

The teachers immediately saw the relevance of the stories to the world they shared with their students. They proved eager to think about the visual images, page layouts, colors, perspectives, and other aesthetic choices the writers and illustrators made, and they were all ready to try their hand at picture-book making themselves. It was clear to the Ciwara teachers that their students needed new and better books in more than just French, but they were not available. The new picture books, while fictional, address real problems in a candid, yet open-ended way.

Because the books are written in Bamanakan, French, and English, the Ciwara teachers can proceed step-by-step to make sure that the students working in small groups can be actively engaged. The first step was for the teacher to read the story from start to finish in Bamanakan while the students followed along in their copies of the book. Occasionally, teachers paused over an unfamiliar word or phrase and asked if any of the students could define it or come up with a synonym.

The teacher also stopped on one of the earlier pages in the book and asked the students what they saw. That is, what strikes them about the image on the page? Is it the colorful clothing, a physical object like the motorcycle that is rendered in fabric, or the posture of one of the characters? Here, the goal is to have the students talk about their own emotional responses to the images or the emotions of the figures in the picture.

Based on their own classroom experiences, the teachers decided that if the students were to discuss their own disagreements about the violent civil war they had been living through, they needed a vocabulary to describe and reflect upon basic and higher-order emotions as well as the skills to make reasonable arguments or counterarguments. This need to address the emotional side of discursive peace building proved to be as important for the teachers as for the students. Both have had experiences similar to the characters in the picture books.

After the first reading, again depending upon the grade level of the students, the teacher asked different students to read the picture book, one page at a time. The younger students read in French, the older ones in French and English.

Once they'd read through the book a second time, discussions began in small groups. The teacher posed a question relating the actions in the picture book to experiences the students may have had themselves. This may be a question about objects, like the motorcycle, that families may cherish because they've lost a loved one they associate with that object. Or, it may be a question about forgiveness or fairness.

After reading and reflecting on the themes and images in the book, the students chose a way of reenacting the story. This may take the form of a dramatic reading, with different students playing different characters in the story. This allows the students to demonstrate that they better understand the relationship between their own emotions and reasons. The goal is not to determine who is right or wrong. The goal is to enable students to understand the opposing reasons and emotions of different figures so that they better understand their own reasons and emotions.

In the following sections of this chapter, two of the picture books will be explored in more detail. These two books highlight the very difficult issues that the teachers wanted the students to have the opportunity to discuss.

CAMP KATI: TRAUMA AND CARE

Philosophical treatments of war and peace have focused primarily on war, leaving the concept of peace relatively underdeveloped until recently. Philosophers have concentrated on just war theory—specifically, what reasons for going to war can be considered moral, what are the moral limits on military conduct in war, and what should and should not be done to remedy the effects of war when the fighting is over?[5] From this perspective, peace is simply the absence of war (for example, peace accords, truces, treaties, and peaceful coexistence). This is what is meant by negative peace.

However, as the violence of war has become better understood, the need for a more positive conception of peace has emerged. The violence of war is not restricted to direct attacks.

There are also structural and cultural forms of violence. Structural violence can include social and economic inequality when it leads to higher mortality rates, especially for infants and women during childbirth, and lower life expectancies for poor people in general. Political disenfranchisement can have similar violent effects on the quality of life.

Cultural violence, while not always as visible as structural and direct violence, also can have significant impacts. The use of racist and sexist language, for example, harms people's self-esteem and makes it more difficult for them to realize their goals, and the threat of violence implicit in public monuments and memorials that celebrate racist ideologies has similar harmful effects. Positive peace building leading to a more democratic culture as well as more democratic political institutions and practices requires the transformation of structures and cultures of violence such as these (Reimer et al. 2015).

Another dimension of the culture of violence that positive peace building addresses involves the traumatic effects of war on survivors.[6] These survivors include combatants, but also noncombatants, on both sides of a conflict.

One particular group of survivors is made up of family members and friends who have lost someone close to them in war. They too can suffer from posttraumatic stress even though they have not been in combat or witnessed direct violence. Positive peace building requires that their trauma be understood and cared for. It is part of a political healing process, not only the care that individuals owe to one another.[7]

The second picture book that was written, *Camp Kati*, deals with a real dilemma faced by the Ciwara students and their peers in Mali (Ouologuem, Cissouma, and Camara 2016). Camp Kati is modeled on the actual Camp Sundiata in Kati, a large military training base named after the legendary national hero and founder of early modern Mali, Sundiata Keita.[8]

Many of the Ciwara students have relatives in the military who have been stationed at Camp Sundiata and deployed in combat zones throughout the country. In the north these government forces were poorly equipped and frequently were the target of terrorist attacks.

The military coup in 2012 originated at Camp Sundiata initially as a protest against the massacre of government forces stationed in the north. Back in Camp Sundiata, a junior army officer and forces loyal to him, encouraged by the wives and mothers of the government soldiers posted in the north, marched the twenty kilometers to the national capital in Bamako and violently occupied the presidential palace after the president and his security forces fled. The coup was soon overturned and its leaders imprisoned.

However, antigovernment forces in the north were emboldened, and this led some of them to move south toward the capital. They were only stopped by an international force led primarily by the former colonial power, France. Since then, an internationally brokered peace accord in 2015 has not been adhered to, and the fighting has spread farther, into areas including a large portion of the central region of the country and neighboring Burkina Faso and Niger.[9]

Salif, the main character in *Camp Kati*, is wrestling with his fear and anger because his father, who is in the military, has been stationed in a region where violent conflicts have broken out (including summary executions of captured government soldiers by insurgents and extremists). The father does return home, but the relationship between the father and his young son is not the same because of the father's traumatic experiences in combat.

Symbolism plays an important role in this picture book. The father's absence is symbolized by his gray motorcycle, which was once colorful but has been unused in his absence. The affection that the boy once felt for his father is symbolized by his soccer shorts, which Salif puts aside as his feelings toward his father change. Their meaning also has faded.

This story was based on actual interviews that the Ciwara teachers and RCAH students conducted with members of families who had lost a father in the civil war. Early in *Camp Kati*, before the father leaves home, father and son are pictured happily riding the father's prized motorcycle together, with Salif wearing his favorite blue shorts (see figure 3.1).

Later in the book, however, Salif assumes a very different posture, alone and without his blue shorts. The Ciwara students are asked to think about body language as well as the off-kilter way that the picture is cropped. What does it mean, for example, that the father's head is not shown in a picture in which he has returned from combat? From whose perspective is this image of the father seen? In addition to discussion and reflection questions such as these, the teachers designed drawing and performance activities that allowed students to express their reactions to the story in different ways, some of them based on the student's own personal experiences.

RCAH students and Ciwara teachers were cautioned to proceed very carefully when discussing these and other questions prompted by *Camp Kati*. The teachers insisted, however, that it was impossible for them to ignore these questions. They argued that many students were coming to school traumatized and that there was no professional help for them.

The teachers argued that the school provided the only safe place to discuss such matters. Obviously, this is a difficult problem and one that was discussed with consultants to remind teachers and RCAH students how fragile some of the Ciwara students could be and the danger of retraumatization.

BUILDING PEACE: RECONCILIATION AND JUSTICE

The fourth picture book produced thus far, *Building Peace*, addresses another side of village life, not the potentially violent conflicts between neighbors but the violent conflict between people who are not part of the same group (Ciwara School Teachers 2017). Transforming these conflicts requires the use of care lest they recur. The disagreements are deeper, sometimes involving historical injustices, and the remedies (reconciliation and compromise) may require *building* new structures that had not existed before, not just *keeping* your word or keeping good neighborly relations intact.

Peace building requires bringing opposing sides together, sometimes after very protracted periods of civil war that have involved military battles, insurgencies, civilian casualties, displacement, and other forms of mass violence, possibly genocide. What kinds of reconciliation are possible under those circumstances? When opposing sides believe that they have legitimate grievances, how can they be reconciled with one another?

It takes time in order to build a rudimentary, just political order. That is, it requires compromise, but it is not always possible to split the difference or agree to disagree.

For example, if a sacred site has been violated or families have been displaced from their homes or traditional lands, it is not easy to find a compromise solution. There are dangers on both sides: granting too much impunity in hope of appeasing the opposition versus committing to harsh punishments for all. Getting half your land back or receiving monetary reparations may be of some value, but it is often not enough to build a positive peace.

Positive peace building is a democratic process of political deliberation, compromise, and reconciliation in order to achieve a just political compromise where none had been before, even where there is no previous conciliatory status quo to which to return. Many actual truth-and-reconciliation processes are ineffective because they wrongly assume that reconciliation means returning to a recently past status quo. In fact, the past is often marked by distributive injustices and other forms of structural and symbolic violence.

The goal of positive peace building is to transform violence into nonviolent forms of political disagreement and deliberation when reconciliation is not available. This may require, for example, that even though all the disputed land may not be returned to its original inhabitants or all the displaced residents may not move back into their former homes, they still can be equal participants in determining how these goods will be valued. Without dividing the land and property in half or otherwise redistributing it, they may recognize through public markers the importance of the disputed land as a heritage site or national monument.

On its face, *Building Peace* is a comic story about a chicken, a homeless bean, and a worm caught in the middle of a fight between the other two (see figure 3.2). Like the other three picture books, *Building Peace* is written in Bamanankan, French, and English. Even though it is written with younger students in mind, students all the way up to grade nine enjoyed discussing which characters they wanted to play, and why. They enjoyed acting out the story, using the picture book as a script read in Bamanankan and then French by one student while others silently portrayed the movements of the characters in a series of tableaux.

The chicken is a favorite among the students because of the way in which she cleans the grounds around her house. The bean, whom the chicken finds sleeping uninvited in her yard, was less popular, though some students felt compassion for him and they identified with his fear of the chicken. The worm is a more complicated figure. His origins were suspect (he emerges from a pile of the chicken's excrement in which the undigested bean also reappears). But several students expressed respect for the worm when at the end of the story he leads the other two quarrelling parties to the village *taguna*.

This is where the story begins to take on more contemporary relevance for the Malian students and their teachers. A *taguna* is a traditional space for peace building found specifically in the Dogon region in Mali. It is basically a building without walls, architecturally designed to equalize political power. Village disputes are brought to the *taguna*, where elders, forced to remain seated by the low thatched roof so that no one can physically command the attention of others, debate the issue or disagreement on its merits.

The chicken asserts an absolute right to property and a basic need for food. The bean, in contrast, is a stranger, possibly displaced by extreme violence elsewhere, which would explain his homelessness, possibly a separatist himself masquerading as a displaced person. The bean implicitly asserts a right to life against the chicken's property rights. The worm emerges out of the chicken's excrement and so has something in common with both of them. He comes from a lowly place like the bean, but it is thanks to the chicken that he is there to lead the other two to the *taguna*, where the conflict can continue without physical violence.

There are several features of traditional Malian culture and history that might enable the three quarreling parties to establish a just compromise.

Students reading and reenacting *Building Peace* benefit from learning about them. One is the tradition of "joking cousins" which can sometimes ease tensions between different ethnic groups otherwise unrelated to each other. As so-called cousins they may adopt a lightheartedness toward one another, even insulting one another in good fun by referring to the other as their slave or servant who should fetch something for them from the market.

Another tradition is that of the griot/griotte or praise singer who can function as a diplomat between opposing political powers. By conveying to both sides the prowess and accomplishments of the other, new mutual respect may be created. One might imagine a student playing the role of the worm acting as a griot/griotte. Or one might imagine the chicken and the bean, instead of ignoring each other in the *taguna*, becoming more like joking cousins than mortal enemies.

Finally, Malian family histories may reveal that the chicken and bean actually have overlapping ethnic roots. It is not unusual for intermarriage to occur across ethnic lines. This may not get them to the *taguna*, but once there, they may discover that a grandparent on one side came from the same ethnic group as the majority of grandparents on the other. This argument is sometimes cited as a reason why Malians are not likely to agree upon some kind of partition to establish a new country of Azawad in the northern territories.[10]

So, even though the chicken has eaten the worm once already and even if the worm is a displaced person from the north, they still may be able to find common ground. That is, there is an opportunity for positive peace building, but it still may be hard to get that conversation started. Students have enjoyed reenacting this story, but their strong preferences for one character over the others seemed to reinforce a belief that one side (the powerful property owner) is right and the other (the homeless person) is wrong. The possibility that there are two sides to the story, even if they are not equally compelling, was not easy for the students to accept.

SIMULATIONS AND DIALOGUES

The goal of all of the picture books has been to prepare students for a political dialogue in which they have to recognize the other legitimate participants and what compromises are permissible and desirable. When understood in this way, perhaps it is not surprising that *Building Peace* was the most challenging picture book for all the Ciwara students. It raises a fundamental question: What constitutes a just peace in situations defined by competing claims about historical injustice?

As the story continues beyond the written page, the chicken may well assert the legitimacy of her wealth and the bean may respond that he has been unjustly displaced and left to scrape out a pitiful existence without support from the national government. This standoff resonates very strongly with the Ciwara students, teachers, and parents. It resembles the long struggle between Tuaregs and other ethnic groups in Mali, and it is one reason for the difficulty mobilizing political support for its Commission for Truth, Justice, and Reconciliation established after the coup and occupation in 2012–2013.

On the other hand, the government has had enormous difficulty bringing insurgent groups into the peace process, which would justify "no impunity" for those who refuse to sign on (Hayner 2018). Other states, such as Algeria, have tried to mediate this process but thus far with no lasting success. The peace process in Mali is still in its early stages, interethnic violence among other ethnic groups such as the Dogon and Fulani is also a serious problem, and the legitimacy of the central government is widely questioned.[11]

One possible way out of this box is to distinguish between acceptable compromises on one hand that fall short of perfect justice but can lead to reconciliation and, on the other hand, unacceptable or "rotten" compromises (i.e., collaboration with the enemy) that are unjust and do not lead to reconciliation. Appeasement is the pejorative term that is reserved for the latter. Avishai Margalit has argued that while peace will require some compromises and even some injustice, rotten compromises that are cruel and humiliating purchase temporary peace at too high a price (2010).

What makes a compromise rotten or likely to rot in the near future, and therefore means it ought to be avoided, is not something that can be calculated with precision in advance. It takes historical knowledge, the ability to recognize family resemblances, and most of all the ability to see things from the perspectives of others.

In *Building Peace*, if the chicken and the bean are to find a just compromise, albeit imperfect, the worm must play an active role. This will not make the conflict between chicken and the bean go away, but it will establish a framework for negotiations under the *taguna* in which the two parties feel they have been recognized as political equals.

The next part of the peace-education program consists of the peace games.

The picture-book project is the first part of a three-pronged peace-building program that is connecting the work in Mali with similar initiatives in mid-Michigan. Alongside the picture books a series of political simulations, the Mali Peace Game, was developed. It is modeled on John Hunter's World Peace Game (Hunter 2014). These simulations introduce principles of democratic self-government through active listening and principled negotiation.

The culmination of these peace-building activities in Mali has been a series of community dialogues in which teachers, student, parents, and other community members are invited to observe a session of the Mali Peace Game and various artistic presentations drawn from the picture books and the games by the students.

They provide the students, first, with an opportunity to present their work to a diverse audience that too often ignores them and then to respond to their comments and questions. Second, they give that audience an opportunity to learn from and communicate with young people on urgent topics. Instead of fearing a "youth bulge" (Filmer and Fox 2014), the goal should be learning how to participate in a national conversation with young people.

CONCLUSION

Corruption is a frequent charge made against the governments of poor, especially newly independent, countries. Whether it takes the form of bribery or extortion and whether it happens on a grand scale or a small one, the assumption is that poor countries lack a tradition of civic virtue. This may partially explain, so the argument goes, the general cynicism about politics and low voter turnout in a country such as Mali. Citizens have low expectations of government officials who have moved up through the ranks through corruption and have made a small fortune (Coulibaly 2013).

Attitudes toward corruption, at least in many African countries, including Mali, are much more nuanced. In a comprehensive survey of thirty-six African countries, published in 2017, a majority of respondents in twenty-three of those countries believed that corruption had increased, but they still felt that citizens could make a difference. Even though 85 percent reported being forced to pay a bribe to public officials, 54 percent believed that citizens could make a difference in reducing government corruption, compared to 34 percent who thought they could not. One of the things that increases citizen confidence in their ability to resist and reduce corruption is education (Isbell 2017).

The causes of the current disarray in the Malian public education system from top to bottom predate the coup of 2012 even though they have been exacerbated by it and its aftermath. There was a nominal return to democracy in 1991 after decades of dictatorial one-party rule and the peaceful succession of power from the first elected president to the second.

Still, Malian citizens have not been able to transform their education system created by the French. They were able to pass an education reform act in 1999 that established bilingual education ("pedagogie convergente") as a priority, but the dominant curriculum still devalues local languages and cultures (Fredo 2004).

While Malians take a great interest in their local affairs, the persistent hierarchical colonial model of education continues to produce mostly passive students. What this suggests is that picture books and political simulations dealing with corruption have their work cut out for them. It also is a reminder of how important such discussions are for peace building in Mali and in other countries, rich and poor, where the norms of democratic citizenship and the fabric of democratic culture have been shredded.

NOTES

1. The peace-education program has truly been a group project. This is especially true of the picture books that have been written and illustrated by teams of Ciwara teachers and RCAH faculty and students. The authors of each of the four books are cited below. The other key partners are Maria Diarra, Deborah Fredo, Chris Worland, and Dave Sheridan.

2. For a review of competing conceptions of peace building, see the material contained on the Interpeace website: https://www.interpeace.org/what-we-do/what-is-peacebuilding/.

3. The term "the long haul" is taken from Horton (1997). Horton's life and work have served as inspirational texts for the work being done in Mali described below.

4. See Groupe Bogolan Kasobane: textile artists, painters, Mali. http://www.africancrafts.com/artist.php?id=groupekasobane. As of July 28, 2018.

5. The locus classicus for this orientation toward war and morality is Walzer (2000). For an expansion that looks at postwar morality from a similar perspective, see Sherman (2015).

6. On the evolution of the social and political meaning of "trauma," see Fassin and Rechtman (2009).

7. For applications of care ethics to politics, see Robinson (1999) and Tronto (2013).

8. For scholarly interpretations of the Sundiata story, see Austen (1999).

9. In 2017, two years after the "Bamako Agreement" was signed in Algiers, many were skeptical it was going to work. See, for example, Boutellis and Zahar (2017). The situation has since become more violent (*Le Monde Afrique*, March 2018).

10. The diehard separatists in Mali are a small minority of the population, even in the north and now central regions. And the specter of separatism in Mali would not be tolerated easily by neighboring countries who would have to deal with similar claims to autonomy by their ethnic minorities. I am indebted to Cheick Oumar Diarrah for discussion on this question of separatism and partition.

11. The U.S. Holocaust Memorial Museum and the Simon-Skjodt Center for Genocide Prevention ranked Mali as the eighth most likely country to devolve into

mass violence in 2016 based on the statistical risk assessment of their Early Warning Project. https://www.earlywarningproject.org/countries/mali.

REFERENCES

Austen, Ralph A., ed. 1999. *In Search of Sunjata: The Mande Oral Epic as History, Literature, and Performance*. Bloomington, IN: Indiana University Press.

Autesserre, Séverine. 2014. *Peaceland: Conflict Resolution and the Everyday Politics of International Intervention.* New York: Cambridge University Press.

Beitz, Charles R. 2011. *The Idea of Human Rights*. New York: Oxford University Press.

Bleck, Jaimie. 2015. *Education and Empowered Citizenship in Mali*. Baltimore, MD: Johns Hopkins University Press.

Boutellis, Arthur, and Marie-Joëlle Zahar. 2017. "Two Years after Bamako Agreement: What Peace Is There to Keep?" *International Peace Institute*. June 22. https://theglobalobservatory.org/2017/06/mali-bamako-agreement-agiers-process-minusma/.

Bratton, Michael. 2016. "Violence, Displacement and Democracy in Post-Conflict Societies: Evidence from Mali." *Journal of Contemporary African Studies* 34, no. 4: 437–58.

Ciwara School Teachers. *Building Peace*. 2017. Illustrated by Joseph Thera and Chris Worland. Kati, Mali: Institute for Popular Education.

Coulibaly, Massa. 2013. "Crise, démocratie et participation, Résultats du round 5 des enquêtes *afrobaromètre*, Enquête au Mali." (March). http://afrobarom eter.org/sites/default/files/media-briefing/mali/mli_r5_presentation1.pdf. As of July 28, 2018.

Coulibaly, Massa, and Moussa Coulibaly. 2018. "Impacts et sequelles de la crise au Mali: psychologiques, economiques, et tenaces." *Afrobarometre*, no. 190 (February): 1–12. http://afrobarometer.org/publications/ad190-impacts-et-sequelles-de-la-crise-au-mali-psychologiques-economiques-et-tenaces. As of July 28, 2018.

Dembele, Moussodjie, Mahamadou Sissoko, and Demba Sissoko. 2016. *The Challenge*. East Lansing, MI : Michigan State University.

Esquith, Stephen L. 2012. "Motivating Responsibility for Children in Poor Countries." In *Child Rights: The Movement, International Law, and Opposition*, edited by Clark Butler. West Lafayette, IN: Purdue University Press.

Fassin, Didier, and Richard Rechtman, eds. 2009. *The Empire of Trauma.* Princeton, NJ: Princeton University Press.

Filmer, Deon, and Louise Fox. 2014. *Youth Employment in Sub-Saharan Africa*. Washington, DC: World Bank.

Fredo, Deborah. 2004. "The Stakes for Quality Education in Mali: 2004." Unpublished manuscript.

Guéhenno, Jean-Marie. 2015. *The Fog of Peace: A Memoir of International Peacekeeping in the 21st Century*. Washington, DC: Brookings Institution.

Hayner, Priscilla. 2018. *The Peacemaker's Paradox: Pursuing Justice in the Shadow of Conflict*. New York: Routledge.
Horton, Myles, with Judith Kohl and Herbert Kohl. 1997. *The Long Haul: An Autobiography*. New York: Teachers College Press.
Hunter, John. 2014. *World Peace and Other 4th Grade Achievements*. New York: First Mariner Books. http://worldpeacegame.org/. As of July 28, 2018.
Isbell, Thomas. 2017. "Efficacy for Fighting Corruption: Evidence from 36 African Countries." *Afrobarometer*. Policy paper no. 21 (July). http://afrobarometer.org. Accessed March 8, 2018.
Levine, Daniel H. 2014. *The Morality of Peacekeeping*. Edinburgh, U.K.: Edinburgh University Press.
Margalit, Avishai. 2010. *On Compromise and Rotten Compromises*. Princeton, NJ: Princeton University Press.
Le Monde Afrique. March 2018. "L'ONU inquiète pour le Mali." https://www.lemonde.fr/afrique/article/2018/03/03/l-onu-inquiete-pour-le-mali_5265055_3212.html.
Moyn, Samuel. 2012. *The Last Utopia: Human Rights in History*. Cambridge, MA: Belknap Press.
Ouologuem, Laya, Kalifa Cissouma, and Mariam Camara. 2016. *Camp Kati*. Illustrated by Laya Ouologuem and Chris Worland. East Lansing, MI: Michigan State University.
Ouologuem, Laya, Marie Samake, Gaston Kone, and Fanta Gakou. *Sekola*. Illustrated by Chris Worland. 2016. East Lansing, MI: Michigan State University.
Reimer, Laura E., Cathryne L. Schmitz, Emily M. Jake, Ali Askerov, Barbara T. Strahl, and Thomas G. Matyok. 2015. *Transformative Change: An Introduction to Peace and Conflict Studies*. Lanham, MD: Lexington Books.
Richmond, Oliver P., and Audra Mitchell, eds. 2012. *Hybrid Forms of Peace: From Everyday Agency to Post-Liberalism*. New York: Palgrave Macmillan.
Robinson, Fiona. 1999. *Globalizing Care: Ethics, Feminist Theory, and International Relations*. Boulder, CO: Westview Press.
Rovine, Victoria L. 2008. *Bogolan: Shaping Culture through Cloth in Contemporary Mali*. 2nd edition. Bloomington, IN: Indiana University Press.
Sherman, Nancy. 2015. *Afterwar: Healing the Moral Wounds of Our Soldiers*. New York: Oxford University Press.
Tronto, Joan C. 2013. *Caring Democracy: Markets, Equality, and Justice*. New York: New York University Press.
Walzer, Michael. 2000. *Just and Unjust War*s*: A Moral Argument with Historical Illustrations*. 3rd edition. New York: Basic Books.
Wartenberg, Thomas E. 2014. *Big Ideas for Little Kids*. 2nd edition. Lanham, MD: Rowman & Littlefield.

Chapter Four

Helping Non-Philosophers Discuss Philosophy with Children

The Rotary Club Project

Ali Bassiri

How can parents or teachers engage children in philosophical discussions? Most adults are not well versed in philosophical topics, and relevant academic books are notoriously difficult to comprehend, let alone apply to everyday conversations. This suggests that a group of adults would have a hard time serving as facilitators of philosophy discussions among schoolchildren.

The present chapter argues that this is not the case. Using facilitators from the Rotary Club of San Jose, most of whom had no prior background in philosophy, a successful program for teaching philosophy in elementary schools was developed. The key was providing the adults with some basic "moves" to use in facilitating a discussion. On the basis of this experience, it is argued that adults without previous philosophical training can work with young children to produce outstanding philosophical discussions.

This chapter outlines the process used to prepare the classroom for a philosophy session and concludes with suggestions for the parent and child reading a storybook at home. Readers interested in greater detail can refer to the book written by the members of the committee on the implementation and outcome of the project (Bassiri et al. 2013).

OVERVIEW OF THE PROGRAM

Inspired and guided by Professor Thomas Wartenberg, the Rotary Club of San Jose (led by Ali Bassiri, a physician with an interest in education, along with a few Rotary members) partnered with the Washington Elementary School (led by principal Maria Evans and teachers Allison Pruitt and Stacy Mascitelli-Morey) and the San Jose State University Philosophy Department (led by Professors Karin Brown and Anand J. Vaidya as well as a group of philosophy students) and formed a committee to develop and implement a philosophy program for second- and third-grade students.

Success was measured subjectively by the degree of engagement of the students. It was implicitly assumed that the lessons learned in implementing philosophy in a classroom could be extrapolated to a parent and child conversing in their living room. So, in addition to developing a philosophy program in two schools, the goal was to provide guidance for parents interested in having philosophical conversations with their children.

The project lasted over two school years, from 2011 to 2013, and used children's storybooks as a catalyst to initiate philosophical discussions. The books used were either chosen from teachingchildrenphilosophy.org or found while browsing local bookstores. In time the project leaders developed a skill for selecting books with potential philosophical content from the large selection of children's books available on the market.

The role of each member on the committee was relatively clear-cut. The professors would provide a philosophical synopsis of the story and prepare the philosophical questions. The teachers would use the synopsis and create a lesson plan appropriate for the students' knowledge levels. Parents and Rotary volunteers would then implement the lesson plan during classroom sessions.

Classroom sessions were conducted once a month and moderated by parents and the Rotary volunteers under the supervision of the teachers. Perhaps the most important role of the committee as a whole was to transform the wording of the philosophical questions so that they were relevant and age appropriate for the children. After each session the teachers would provide feedback, which served as the basis for quality improvement of subsequent lesson plans.

The project initially started with two schools: a private elementary school in a relatively affluent part of San Jose, and a public school in an underprivileged part of the city with a large Mexican community. Professor Wartenberg made an appearance at both schools early on and moderated a demonstration session for all committee members to observe. Parents served as the volunteer moderators for the private school whereas Rotary volunteers conducted the public school sessions.

Unfortunately, the public school parents were not as involved as the private school parents. Many did not speak English well and in general did not have the same education level as the private school parents. These parents were not in the same position to moderate classroom sessions or to replicate the classroom sessions at home. The latter was one of the initial goals of the project that unfortunately was never realized (see below).

In general, the committee had less control over the sessions at the private school. The private school parents often deviated from the lesson plan, improvised, and often assumed the role of a teacher as opposed to a moderator. Traditionally instruction involves the unilateral flow of information from the teacher to the student. A moderator seeks to get children to interact with one another, so that the flow of information circulates among the children. It was this role that the parents found hard to adopt. Most of them had master's or doctorate degrees and most held strong opinions about the issues discussed. In one particular session two parents actually got into an argument in front of the class!

The teachers at the private school also never bought into the project and held the view that critical thinking is already being taught in their classrooms. After a few months their principal decided to abandon the sessions, and the project continued thereafter only at the public school. This was a great loss, as the private school parents were in a favorable position to take the lessons to their homes, read with their children, and report their experience to the committee.

Since the goal of the project was to discover how to engage children in philosophical discussions and not to necessarily teach philosophy topics, it was felt that the project could proceed without the private school involvement. On the positive side, the committee now had far greater control of the content and the moderation of the sessions.

RESULTS

By the end of the second year the group had created a method that was successful in engaging children in philosophical discussions. Two core principles formed the basis of this method:

- transform the role of the students from passive learners to active participants
- transform the role of the adult from "informed leader" to the "uninformed questioner"

To achieve these goals, active learning methods were used which included role play and skits as adults mingled with children "playing dumb" and asking questions such has "help me out here, what is happiness? Or "tell me, why do we make mistakes?"

During the two years of engaging children in philosophical discussion, we learned a great deal about how to make sessions succeed. Here are the basic steps for doing so that were garnered through trial and error during the classroom sessions:

1) Create age-appropriate philosophical questions
One of the most important tasks, if not *the* most important task, in preparing for a successful discussion is the transformation of classic philosophical questions into ones a child readily understands. Take the question "Can we trust our senses to provide accurate knowledge of reality?" This question is too abstract for children (and in fact most adults!). The same question can be presented as "Why do we make mistakes?" This latter question is not the exact same philosophical question but close enough to initiate a discussion on the nature of knowledge.

Continuing with the topic of knowledge as an example, the book *Morris the Moose* by Bernard Wiseman was used to stimulate classroom discussion. In the book, Morris encounters a variety of animals whom he believes are all moose like himself. Only when he sees a reflection of himself and a cow in a lake does he understand that he's made a mistake. Sample questions used were: "Why did Morris make a mistake?"; "Why do people make mistakes?"; and "Is there anything you can do to make sure you don't make a mistake?" These questions are within the grasp of children and allow them to reflect on assumptions they have made about what they know and whether they might be mistaken about their claims to possess knowledge.

In general, it is important not to strive for philosophical perfection. It is better to be overly simplified and lose some of the philosophical sophistication than to be near-perfect academically. The central goal is to pose questions that the children can grasp. If a question is incomprehensible to the children, the session will never get off the ground. Teachers and involved parents are in a good position to identify age-appropriate questions. At the end, however, there's no substitute for direct classroom or living room experience in learning how to modify questions to stimulate a child.

2) Make the philosophical questions relevant to the child's life
Relevance is another crucial element of an age-appropriate question. Elementary school children in general are not able to understand allegory or symbolism as easily as adults. They are less likely to be able to extrapolate the relevance of a story to their own lives. As a result, great effort needs to be made to re-create questions within the context of the child's everyday life. Such contexts include playground politics, homelife, afterschool activities, and classroom dramas, among others.

An example is a question on friendship based upon "Alone," one of the stories in Arnold Lobel's book *Days with Frog and Toad*. In the story, Frog sits alone on an island contemplating how lucky he is. His friend Toad watches from a distance, thinking his friend is upset at him, and wonders if he should respect his privacy or approach him. The story touches on issues of friendship and privacy, but Toad and Frog may not fully engage the child. An analogy is a child sitting by himself in a playground. Should he be left alone or approached? Once again, teachers and parents can identify appropriate analogies to stimulate discussion.

3) Use active learning methods and incorporate physical movement
Passive learning methods, where the adult asks a question and the seated student answers, are too reminiscent of a typical classroom and can easily cause the children to lose interest. Such a style usually elicits a response from a few vocal students while the silent majority drift off. Although more relevant to the classroom than the living room, it is always preferable to incorporate active learning methods when a group of children are involved. Active learning methods include skits, role play, small-group discussions, and group debate where students discuss issues with each other and the adults are equal participants in the discussion.

In general, the student should be doing about 90 percent of the talking and the adult should spend about 90 percent of the time listening. All too often this ratio is reversed and passive learning dominates. Part of becoming an experienced moderator is not just posing the relevant questions but also stepping back and allowing the children to carry the discussion. It is equally important to teach the children to listen while other children are talking. Too often the children are so focused on the adults that they don't listen to their classmates when they are talking.

To make all this happen, prior to classroom sessions the teachers prepared the class with a review of "Rules of Doing Philosophy":

- Listen respectfully when it's another person's turn to speak
- Raise your hand and wait to be acknowledged before speaking
- Be respectful of other people's opinions

Teacher Allison Pruitt also added "Procedures" to her pre-class instructions:

- Listen carefully to what is being said
- Think about whether you agree with it or not
- Think of reasons to back up your opinion
- Disagree respectfully

It goes without saying, however, that adults must model these behaviors in class.

Incorporating "movement breaks," where every ten to fifteen minutes students are allowed to stand up and move around the classroom, helps children maintain their focus. In general, children have a difficult time standing or sitting still for prolonged periods. Movement helps children regain mental energy and retain focus. Many students are kinesthetic learners, and movement helps their comprehension of didactic material.

4) Make adults participants and not instructors

Children usually assume that adults have all the answers to the questions being posed. As such, they may be less likely to get engaged with questions and await the presentation of the "correct answer" by the adult. Children will respond much more enthusiastically if adults "play dumb" and ask the children to help them answer questions. Socrates often is presented as striking just such a pose when he interacts with his fellow Athenians, so this strategy has a venerable philosophical history.

An example of how one might do this is to ask the children, "Help explain this to me. I don't quite understand. What could happen if I lie to my mom and say I did my homework so I can watch cartoons?" Children usually are eager to jump in and offer their opinions if they feel they are helping an ignorant adult.

One of the most important intellectual tools available to the adult is to make the child address the consequences of their answers. This requires some basic philosophical knowledge on the part of the adult. For example, if the child answers, "Yes, it's ok to lie to Mom so I can watch cartoons," the moderator can continue to play dumb and ask, "Well, what happens if one day she catches you?" This question will generate a lively discussion and can be followed up by asking, "Do you think your mom would believe you the next time you said you had done your homework?" Discussion can subsequently focus on such philosophical topics as the value of trust, the importance of promise keeping, trustworthiness, and honesty in the family, among friends, and perhaps in society in general (a topic that can be broached by asking about the role of trust in their school).

5) Prepare a lesson plan

Lesson plans have been well described in Wartenberg's book *Big Ideas for Little Kids* (2009). Our template for a classroom lesson plan was as follows:

- Small-group discussion: discuss a question relevant to child's life
- Role play / Skit: adults perform a short skit re-creating the question
- Group debate: class discussion related to the story or skit
- Fishbowl: students lead a discussion on what they learned

For example, on the topic of authority, aesthetics, and justice we held a drawing contest in the classroom. The judge (Professor Brown) purposely chose a lesser drawing as the winner, much to the protest of the students. This action re-created the plot of *Emily's Art* by Peter Catalanotto, a book the students had read beforehand.

This session was very successful in engaging the students to come up with what criteria should be used to judge art and what qualifies someone to act as a judge. Most memorable was how the children approached the "judge" in as respectful a manner as they contested her (clearly wrong) decision. The judge could barely hide her smile and how proud she was of these children challenging her authority.

Our sessions usually ended with a "Fishbowl," composed of about seven chairs arranged in a circle with one student leading the discussion on what they learned that day. Students (and adults) take turns occupying a chair, summarizing their conclusions, and vacating the seat for the next individual. Fishbowl is perhaps the best indicator of how successful a session has been. If discussions are lively and students eager to occupy a seat, then the session was a success. Fishbowl is also an indirect method to obtain feedback from the children on the impact of these sessions on their learning.

Parents wishing to explore a story with their child at their own home are unlikely to spend the effort to make a lesson plan. What can be very helpful, though, is for them to have a basic working knowledge of philosophical issues such as "Why is truthfulness better than deceit?" or "How can our senses mislead us?" An uninformed parent is less likely to have a productive discussion with a child. Both our book and most of Professor Wartenberg's books make extra efforts to explain philosophical issues in a simple fashion with relevant real-life examples. Parents are encouraged to invest the extra time and develop a basic working knowledge of the philosophical topics she or he will discuss with her child(ren).

Using the concept of friendship as an example, here are a few intellectual tools parents can use when reading stories with their children. These tools explore epistemology (the theory of knowledge), aesthetics (the philosophy of beauty), ontology (the nature of being), ethics, and identity among other topics and can be used to make everyday discussions more philosophical.

- *Find commonalities* among examples:
  What do all your friends have in common?
- *Identify* the most important quality of an example:
  What's the most important thing about your friends? About you?
- Describe the *perfect example*, what philosophers call "a paradigm":
  Describe the perfect friendship. What makes an ideal friend?
- Ask for *counterexamples*:
  Do you have a friend who is not funny or popular?

- List the *pros and cons*:
  Should you help a friend who's being bullied? What are reasons to help them? What are reasons not to?
- Ask for *objective criteria* when comparing things:
  List everything that can make a good friend? Or a bad friend?
- Ask children to *give reasons* for their views:
  Why do you say that? How do you know?

There are other tools such as encouraging proper reasoning and pointing out logical fallacies, but they are more advanced and require a commitment of time and learning on the part of the adult. The basic ones listed here will allow a parent to have a productive philosophical discussion with a child or children.

6) Start with the concrete and move to the abstract
As has already been pointed out, the engagement of children with philosophy proceeds best when it begins with simple, concrete questions taken from storybooks or everyday life. To choose a hypothetical example, say that the topic to be discussed is happiness and the story to be used features a girl, Jane, who appears happy. In order to have a fruitful discussion, the moderator might proceed to ask the children the following questions sequentially:

a) "Jane seems happy. Why do you think she's happy?"
b) "What makes you happy?"
c) "Is there something that makes you happy all the time, even when not doing it?"

The idea here is that the abstract questions characteristic of philosophy cannot just be presented to the children without some preliminary warm-up.

The first question is purely concrete and taken from the hypothetical story. It introduces the topic in a manner that doesn't require the children to do more than pay attention to what they have heard and think about it using a specific concept central to the discussion. As such, it serves as a springboard for the next question.

The second question focuses on the children's own experience and asks them to state their own opinions about things that make them happy. To this point, no philosophy has been done, even if the results of the children's reflections are interesting.

It is only with the third question that the children are invited into the world of abstract thinking. But even here, the connection to the children's own experience remains central. In answering this question, the children are beginning to distinguish those things that make you happy in a particular context, like eating a donut, from those that make you happy even outside of a specific context, like parental love. This philosophical distinction may not be possible with second and third graders, nonetheless, the answers they put forward are often quite profound.

Some books naturally invite abstract discussions. *The Important Book* by Margaret Wise Brown explores the topic of "essential properties" by listing the fundamental characteristics of a number of objects. Children readily participate in discussions of "What's the most important thing about an apple?" or "What's the most important thing about you?" Once these questions have been explored, one can ask "What makes you, you?" or "Is there something about you that will never change?" Children readily dive into these difficult philosophical questions because they involve the most relevant person in their lives, themselves!

7) Make it fun!
Perhaps most importantly, philosophy should be fun. It should be reiterated to the child that there are no right or wrong answers and certainly the child should feel comfortable that he or she is not being judged on the "correctness" of her answers. When children feel they are not being judged, they tend to open up and share their opinions. It is important as well to continually encourage the child with remarks such as "That's a great answer!" or "Boy, that was a smart comment!" By the end of the project, the students were quite eager to take part in these philosophy sessions, partly because it was a nonthreatening avenue to voice their opinions.

REFLECTIONS

As mentioned before, there's no substitute for experience, and there's definitely a learning curve in acquiring the skill of engaging children in philosophy. The benefits, however, are well worth the effort. A few anecdotes will demonstrate some of our experiences in this field, both positive and negative:

- During a session on judging the merits of two drawings, one girl insisted on drawing A being superior and gave appropriate reasons while everyone else in the class favored drawing B. The moderators did an excellent job of stimulating the discussion, which basically pitted one student against the rest of the class. The session ended with everyone having voiced their opinions respectfully and intellectually.

    Afterward, the principal, almost ecstatic, commented about this girl who apparently had an extremely difficult home situation with a single mom who worked the streets: "This is the only time I have ever heard her speak this much all year. She was so proud and confident. She will remember this class forever!" Sometimes the student who benefits most from philosophy is the one we least expected to speak up.

- During a session on justice the moderator asked the class to come up with an example of something that's not fair. A little boy raised his hand: "I don't think it's fair that we don't have enough to eat at home." Jolted, the moderator had to take a few seconds to compose herself and fight back tears. She continued on with directing the conversation on how studying, getting an education and a good job will prevent this in the future. When we recounted this story to the dean at San Jose State University, however, she could not hold back her tears!

    This example demonstrates that philosophy discussions encourage students to be more forthcoming than they would generally be in their classrooms. Perhaps because of the nonjudgmental nature of our philosophy sessions, this boy felt he could talk about his difficulties at home without fear of being shamed.

- During another session, the discussion on justice got a bit animated and one of the kids spontaneously blurted out, "If someone killed my dad I would go and kill their dad." His classmate quickly and passionately replied, "Well, now you have left him without a father too. What good is that?" The moderator was unsure whether this student had lost his father through violence (as this school was situated in a high-crime neighborhood of San Jose). The response, however, was intelligent and seemed to be readily grasped by everyone, as no one offered a counterargument.

- The most traumatic session for the moderators occurred during the early part of the second year. The topic was lying, and the moderators adapted one of Kant's examples. In response to the statement, "It is never acceptable to lie," Kant asked what you would do if a madman with an axe is searching to kill your friend and asks you his whereabouts. Would you tell the truth and see your friend killed? Against our expectations, Kant argued that lying was always wrong.

    To re-create this question, the moderators pretended a bully is outside looking for one of the kids in the classroom. We hid the "targeted" student behind a curtain and started to create drama about whether we all should lie to the bully or not when he comes into the class. The principle moderator suddenly noticed that the class had become absolutely silent. He looked around and three children were clinging to the teacher's legs in tears. The session was immediately stopped.

    It quickly dawned on everyone that the Sandy Hook massacre had taken place a few days prior and the country was still in shock. The adults spent the rest of the class pacifying the children and reassuring them that this was all make-believe and there really was no bully outside. Surprisingly the principal was extremely calm when she heard about the incident, made a few phone calls, and nothing untoward ever came out of the incident nor were there any residual effects on the students.

The committee members, however, were quite shaken and decided that (1) with rare exceptions, children would no longer be included in the skits, (2) extreme care would be exercised regarding what types of skits are performed in class, avoiding any that could have potential negative consequences, and (3) it would be made absolutely clear to the children at the beginning of a session that this is all make-believe.

No matter whether these provided adequate responses to the situation, everyone became aware that philosophy discussions had the potential to be quite upsetting to students, so that extreme care needed to be used in preparing the sessions.

What the above examples show is the value philosophy can bring to a child's life. When conducted properly such that children do not feel judged, an environment of trust and an intellectually open community is created. When children feel safe they open up and share personal concerns and beliefs, and a bond of respect is created between the adult and the child. In contrast, if done carelessly, the consequences can be stifling and traumatic, with children closing up and refusing to participate. Philosophy through children's literature can be an invaluable tool for parents looking for ways to communicate with their children.

CONCLUSION

The Washington Elementary School Philosophy Project was inspired by the work of Professor Wartenberg. An unintended consequence of the project of bringing philosophy to young children was the engagement of adults with philosophy. All the non-philosophers involved with this project (including the teachers and principal) felt more confident in their ability to tackle philosophical topics and their ability to take any story, delve deeper than just the superficial plot, and engage a child in a meaningful discussion. In the end, the project turned out to be about the intellectual growth of both the children and the adult moderators. All of the participants benefited from taking part in the project, and the effects of their participation will hopefully continue to be felt in every aspect of their lives.

REFERENCES

Bassiri, A., K. Brown, M. Evans, S. Mascitelli-Morey, A. Pruitt, A. J. Vaidya, T. E. Wartenberg. 2013. *Implementing Philosophy in Elementary Schools: The Washington Elementary School Philosophy Project.* Bloomington, IN: AuthorHouse.
Brown, Margaret Wise. 1999. *The Important Book.* New York: HarperCollins.
Catalanotto, Peter. 2001. *Emily's Art.* New York: Atheneum Books.
Lobel, Arnold. 1979. *Days with Frog and Toad.* New York: Harper & Row.
Wartenberg, Thomas E. 2009. *Big Ideas for Little Kids: Teaching Philosophy through Children's Literature.* Lanham, MD: Rowman & Littlefield.
Wiseman, Bernard. 1991. *Morris the Moose.* New York: HarperCollins.

Chapter Five

High School Goes to Kindergarten and Beyond

Mitchell Bickman and Laura Trongard

At the earliest stages of schooling children are ripe for philosophical inquiry. As children develop, they are trying to make sense of the world as they experience things for the first time, so to them asking questions is a natural part of their development.

How often have we witnessed children, perhaps our own, asking questions almost to the point of annoyance? Such questioning was recently on display on a train ride into Manhattan. A father and son were discussing their visit to the American Museum of Natural History. The two began discussing the dinosaur bones they would see at the museum. It spurred no fewer than twenty questions as to why dinosaurs are extinct.

The father shared a somewhat sanitized version of the dinosaurs' extinction, and he briefly mentioned the role meteorites might have played. Given the nature of the previous discussion, one would assume that this new topic would lead to twenty new questions, but surprisingly the boy instantly knew what meteorites were. Seemingly shocked, the father asked how his young son—who seemed to be no older than four—knew what meteorites were. The boy responded, "From Doc McStuffins." Given the boy's age, this was presumably one of his most beloved teachers.

This child, along with elementary-school-aged students across our nation, are *divergent thinkers* whose natural sense of wonder is something we often take for granted. Divergent thinkers are individuals (often children) who typically think out of the box, finding creative or unorthodox ideas/solutions to problems that they encounter. Young children's thought processes are typically more open-ended than adults' as they have not gone through years of formal schooling where over time students become more *convergent thinkers* as schooling often values singular right answers.

That is the beauty of philosophy where singular "correct" answers do not exist. Through philosophical questioning, we can tap into children's natural abstract thinking and begin to provide a framework for helping students to develop reasoning skills.

BIG IDEAS FOR LITTLE KIDS

Oceanside is a K–12 public school on Long Island's South Shore with a student population of six thousand. In reflecting on our curricula across multiple disciplines, we noticed a gap in students' education as philosophical instruction was largely nonexistent. Unfortunately, this is common in many elementary schools due to the ever-increasing demands within core subjects and testing. This was concerning to us, as philosophy provides an important foundation for fostering students' thinking skills, reasoning, questioning, and other habits of mind that philosophy instills in students.

In addition, by integrating philosophical instruction, we are able to explore the natural connections that exist between disciplines, allowing us to teach a more cohesive narrative. It has enabled us to slowly break down the traditional silos that separate schooling into discipline-specific instruction where students learn math, science, English, and social studies as separate and distinct entities, missing out on the connections between each discipline that when explored in concert with one another strengthen students' metacognitive skills.

Oceanside is now in its fourth year of a program called Big Ideas for Little Kids, borrowing our title from Thomas Wartenberg's book by the same name, where our high school students teach philosophy to elementary students in grades K–6 by pushing into on average sixty-plus classrooms three times a year. This chapter details our program from its early inception, initially working with kindergarten students, to its growth and expansion over time, where philosophical instruction in now delivered in every elementary grade.

The chapter's focus is on how we train high school students to do this work, as our high school students are at the heart of this program. It will also share insights from our experiences, as well as provide an overview of the learning outcomes we have witnessed in both our high school philosophical trainers as well as in our elementary students. Ultimately, the goal of our program is to build a strong foundation for questioning so that students become critical consumers of their world.

Professor Wartenberg has worked with children of all ages, but his research resonated most with us for our kindergarten students. Over time we have expanded our initial work, growing the program in grades K–6. Wartenberg's program at Mount Holyoke College utilized college students in his introduction to philosophy class to deliver philosophy lessons to second-grade students via the lens of picture books. In Oceanside, we adapted the framework that Wartenberg developed to fit the needs of our students at both the high school and elementary levels.

One of the first hurdles we encountered was that we did not have a formal, or informal for that matter, philosophy class to tap into to disseminate this work. After considerable dialogue amongst teachers and administrators, we settled on using high school sophomores to be our turnkey philosophical trainers who would eventually be the ones to push into elementary school to deliver philosophy lessons to our youngest of students, as students' sophomore year is often less stressful than their junior and senior years, when they have an eye toward the college admissions process.

The sophomores we chose to be philosophy facilitators in the Big Ideas for Little Kids program were part of an integrated program that allowed them to take part in field trips to elementary schools without missing other classes. Our integrated program is a three-period humanities block where students go from English to social studies, and have an additional third-period class, which is called conferencing, that meets every other day. Philosophical instruction is a great fit for conference because it can help students become critical consumers of information, encourage questioning, and promote using evidence to support ideas.

The second way in which Oceanside's program differed from that of Professor Wartenberg is that we decided to first deliver philosophical instruction not to our upper elementary students, but to our youngest of students in kindergarten. While we would like to tell you that we wanted an additional challenge, or based our decision on research about the benefits of introducing philosophy to children from the time they begin to question their world, the decision was slightly more selfish in that both of us had three- and four-year-old children at home who were perfect test subjects for this work.

PHILOSOPHICAL INQUIRY WITH CHILDREN

To engage in philosophical inquiry, children do not need to understand the ideas of history's greatest philosophers. What they do need is their natural inquisitiveness and the willingness to take part in an ongoing dialogue. The best place to start is with something that they have already had great exposure to: picture books. Picture books provide a natural point of entry where students can begin to dissect, wrestle with, and discuss big ideas and questions that surround them in their lives.

Before piloting the program in classrooms, we first facilitated philosophical discussions with three- and four-year-old children to see if it could work. One of the books we read was *The Important Book*, which raises the question of whether everything that exists has an essential property. On each page, the author describes a few properties of an object and ends each page with a claim about which property is the most important.

At first, the children we read to were inclined to agree with the author's claims and took the stance that anything written in a book must be true. However after a couple pages and a few philosophical questions, the children realized that it was acceptable to challenge the book and have their own ideas. When asked if there is one "most important" thing about apples, one three-year-old child responded that she would have to learn more about apples before making her decision.

It quickly became clear that children as young as three are ready to have philosophical conversations and can develop skills that are taught in higher grade levels. We were ready to begin an ambitious and exciting program that we were confident with in theory but unsure about in practice.

Before we fully fleshed out the design of Oceanside's philosophy program we decided to do a small-scale test run at our Kindergarten Center. After holding several meetings with a focus group of kindergarten teachers and the principal of the Kindergarten Center in Oceanside, a plan was devised to work with two different kindergarten classes for two sessions each before bringing the program to the whole school. The first session would be an ethical philosophical discussion and the second session would be a discussion based on a children's book.

In the first session, students were introduced to the rules of what Wartenberg calls the "Game of Philosophy." Like any game, our philosophical discussions were governed by a set of ground rules that allow the students to play the Game of Philosophy. These included how to conduct oneself, how to make a contribution to the discussion, and how to appropriately agree or disagree with classmates.

In going over the rules of the Game of Philosophy, it became apparent that the kindergarten students viewed disagreement in a negative way, so the facilitators modeled an example of how to disagree respectfully with each other. It was important for kindergarten students to realize that it is not mean or wrong to disagree as long as it is done in a respectful way.

After reviewing ground rules, we posed an introductory philosophical topic that students could debate. For this exercise, the topic can be any short scenario that allows the students to engage in philosophical discussion while practicing the rules. In our case it was the following:

High School Goes to Kindergarten and Beyond   71

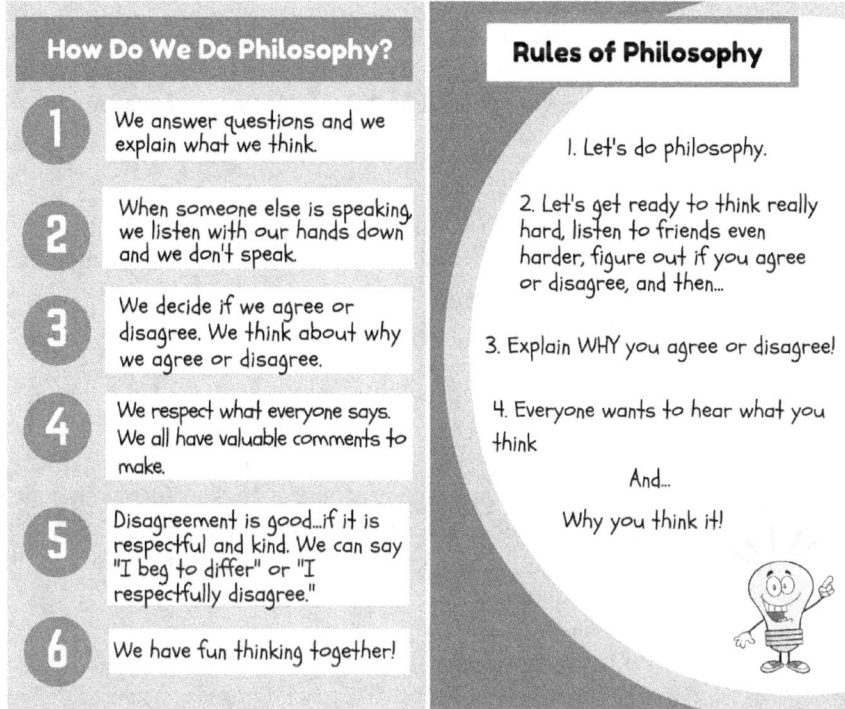

Figure 5.1. Rules Poster

"Imagine you go into a candy store and see all of your favorite candies there. Would it be ok to take something without paying if you knew that you would never be caught?"

Through this first session we learned divergent thinking, which is commonplace in very young children, also has defined limits with regards to following rules and laws. This was exemplified by the hypothetical scenario above we choose to model with students. The following is a sampling of their responses:

Student 1—No, it would not be ok.

Facilitator—Why?

Student 1—Because the store would have a camera and you would be caught later.

Facilitator—Ok, but remember that you will not be caught in this scenario.

Student 2—No, not ok because if the store didn't have a camera, the worker at the store would have a cell phone and tape you and then you would be caught.

Student 3—No, it is not ok to take something without paying.

Facilitator—Why?

Student 3—Because when you left the store there would be a policeman waiting outside and you would be arrested.

Facilitator—As a reminder, you will NOT be caught.

Student 4—It's not ok because when you go home your mommy and daddy will see a candy wrapper in the garbage and they didn't buy it for you so you will get in trouble.

Facilitator—Guys, in this story you will NOT BE CAUGHT.

Finally after the fourth student shared his response, Tessa, a kindergartner, said "No, it is not ok." We asked Tessa why it was not ok. She responded by saying stealing is wrong. It was at that moment that something magical happened. There was an evolution in thinking where it clicked for all students with her peers adding on to her response. We found out in this session that kindergartens' moral sense of rules, laws, and what is right and wrong is deeply ingrained at this young age.

Our first session ended by having a go-round, where each student shared something he or she learned from our time with them. Coincidentally, in the go-round we made it to our last student, Mikey, who proudly declared, "I've stolen twice before." We asked Mikey if this was a good or bad decision? His response: "Stealing is very bad and I will never do it again." To this day we never found out what Mikey stole, but hopefully he left his young life of crime behind him due to his enlightenment from our philosophical conversation.

Upon reflecting on our initial experience we learned that it was best to start out the philosophy program with a discussion based on a children's book rather than to pose a simple ethical question like we had done. Posing the question about stealing was problematic in two ways.

First off, there are no right answers during a philosophical discussion, and the facilitators should not pull students in any particular direction or look for any particular answer. However, in the discussion of stealing, facilitators were hoping for a specific outcome: for students to discuss *why* stealing is wrong. Another problem is since facilitators are not supposed to guide or praise any answers, you run the risk of kindergarten students leaving the session with the wrong idea, in this case about stealing. Our goal is to have students question their world and think critically but not necessarily challenge laws at the tender age of five.

The next session of the test run involved a philosophical discussion based on a popular children's book. The kindergarten students were drawn into the discussion via the vivid pictures and the story. At different points in the book, students were excited to make guesses as to what would happen next. The pictures helped students stay focused on the story and gave them a chance to analyze visuals. During the discussion, students were able to make evidence-based claims by using parts of the story. If the discussion went too far off track, the facilitator could refer back to the book to bring the conversation back on topic.

As we wrapped up the test run, we began making modifications and training materials to prepare our high school sophomores to be turnkey facilitators in the program.

TRAINING PHILOSOPHICAL FACILITATORS

A brief overview of the field of philosophy was provided to high school students at the start of the training process. High school students analyzed definitions of philosophy and discussed the importance of asking questions in the learning process. Next these same students played a game called "Philosophy or Not Philosophy" in which they had to decide whether questions could be classified as philosophical or not. A question is philosophical when it is one that cannot be answered empirically and for which no specific discipline has been developed that is capable of providing an answer to it. The following are sample questions used in the game.

- What does it mean to be a friend?
- Is it raining out?
- Do you need to be sad sometimes in order to be happy other times?
- What equipment is needed to play baseball?

Bringing in the element of a game and letting the class debate whether or not a question is philosophical not only helped students grasp what philosophy is but also made them excited about the program. Students wanted to get into deep discussion about questions such as "Do you need to be sad sometimes in order to be happy other times?" rather than move on to categorizing the next question.

During the next training session, we modeled reading a book aloud and facilitating a philosophical conversation with the high school students. Students practiced using the language of the Game of Philosophy, listening to each other, explaining their thoughts, and ending with a "go round." This step was repeated with each book before it was used in the kindergarten classrooms so that the high school students had a chance to be a participant in the conversation and think deeply about the questions raised by the book.

The next step was to have high school students practice leading philosophical discussions. In order to do this a fishbowl method was used. The fishbowl method calls for half of the class to sit in an inner circle of desks and participate in a discussion while the other half of the class sits in an outer circle observing the discussion so that they can provide feedback and share ideas when the discussion is over. In this particular fishbowl, students in the inner circle were to have a philosophical discussion based on a children's book.

Two students in the inner circle were chosen to be the facilitators and the rest of the group were the participants. In order to prepare the high school students for different types of learners and personalities that they might encounter in the kindergarten classroom, the following roles were assigned to some of the participants.

Quiet Student: You are a shy student who does not volunteer answers. You participate when called on but you speak softly and do not give long answers.
Talkative Student: You love participating in discussions. You raise your hand very often because you always have something to say.
Interruptive Talkative Student 2: You love participating in discussions. Sometimes you share your answer without being called on because you get so excited about sharing your thoughts.
Off-Track Student: You like to participate. Sometimes your answers seem to come from left field.
Distracted Student: You love to stare out the window during class. Although you are usually not paying attention, you join in when the teacher (facilitator) calls on you and brings you into the discussion.

As the inner circle had a philosophical discussion based on the book, students in the outer circle wrote down any issues they identified during the discussion, strategies that they noticed the facilitators used, and what went well, as well as any suggestions or ideas they had for improvement. Jotting down notes helped the outer circle provide constructive feedback for the inner circle when the discussion was over.

At this point in the training, the high school teachers shared some basic teaching strategies to help the students facilitate discussion. One of the most important strategies for philosophy is using "wait time." Wait time is the period of silence between when a question is asked and when a student is called on to respond. It is important for all students to have time to process the question asked and formulate a response. If the teacher or facilitator calls on a student too quickly, not everyone will have had enough time to think, and odds are they might end up agreeing with the first answer since they have not come up with their own. Although the silence may seem uncomfortable at first, our high school students were able to master the technique and recognized the importance of giving students time to think.

The rules of the Game of Philosophy can be used as a tool to help high school students with classroom management. If students are calling out answers or talking over one another, the facilitators remind everyone that the rules state, "When someone else is speaking, we listen with our hands down and we don't speak" and "We respect what everyone says. We all have valuable comments to make." If students are quiet and reticent about participating, the facilitators remind them that there are no right or wrong answers. The rules say, "Everyone wants to hear WHAT you think and WHY you think it."

During philosophy sessions, both high school and elementary students wear name tags. Being able to call on students by name helped to create a comfortable, familial environment that promoted participation even during the first session. Kindergarten students used each other's names when they participated by saying, "I agree with Student X or I respectfully disagree with Student X." Knowing the students' names also helped facilitators keep the group on track. If a student was distracted or disruptive, facilitators were able to call on them or use their name as they were speaking as an effective way to bring the distracted student back into the conversation.

We have found the ideal use of physical space for discussion is for high school students to be on the same level as the kindergarten students. This is easily achieved by having all students sit in a circle on the floor. In this arrangement, high school students do not seem intimidating to younger students and appear to be more of a co-learner than a teacher. High school students are encouraged to spread out in the circle because the kindergarten students actively engage, improve their focus, and often self-correct their behavior when they have a facilitator physically close to them.

The last step before going into the kindergarten classrooms is for students to meet in groups to prep and develop a "game plan." This entails high school students dividing up jobs, practicing reading the book aloud, developing additional philosophical questions, and setting goals for the group. When reading the books, high school students practice reading slowly, being animated, and varying the level of their voice to captivate young learners.

Developing philosophical questions during prep time for each session helps students think philosophically and take some ownership of the program. High school students have a sense of pride from developing thought-provoking questions. Their questions have proven to be successful in part because they are able to tailor questions to the interests of the kindergarten audience. For example, when discussing the concept of bravery in "Dragons and Giants," high school students wrote questions about superheroes and characters from the movie *Frozen.* These are two beloved topics of the kindergarten students, so the questions sparked a passionate debate. Below are other sample questions developed by students about bravery.

- Does getting a shot at the doctor's office require bravery?
- Do you have to be brave to ride on a roller coaster?
- Do you need to be brave to participate in class?

To create a "game plan" students pick which question they plan on asking first and discuss a possible order of questions. Even though they develop a plan, students are reminded to be flexible with the order of questions and direction of the conversation once it begins. It is important to let the conversation flow naturally and for the students to feel comfortable asking unplanned questions in the moment. Students should not rush through questions or feel like they have to ask every question. Students are aware that the conversation can be very different in each classroom as each student has their own ideas and questions that shape the direction of each conversation.

Goal setting is an important component in the training process. Before each visit to the Kindergarten Center, high school students set both individual goals and group goals. In order to set group goals, group members reflect on what went well in the previous session and what areas could use improvement. Goals are never about getting a specific answer during a session but rather pertain to ensuring that high school students create a safe and relaxed environment in which kindergarteners feel comfortable sharing their ideas and questions.

THE PHILOSOPHY SESSIONS

Between four to six high school students are assigned to each kindergarten classroom. The group starts off presenting together for the introduction and rules and then breaks up so that two to three high school students run a discussion with half of the kindergarten students in the class. The high school students start off the first session by introducing themselves and going over the rules of the Game of Philosophy. Since many kindergarten students perceive disagreement in a negative way, high school students model a respectful disagreement. The following disagreement is provided by high school students as a sample.

Student 1: Grass is brown.

Student 2: I beg to differ. Grass is not brown! Grass is green!

Student 3: I agree with Student 2 that grass is green. Think about the field we play on at recess. The grass is green.

Student 1: I respectfully disagree with Students 2 and 3. I do not think that grass has to be green. I was walking my dog yesterday and noticed that my neighbor's grass is brown. It was crunchy when I walked on it and it did not look green at all.

Student 2: Actually, I know what you are talking about. I have changed my mind because I think if grass is dying it is no longer green. I think grass can be brown sometimes.

After modeling the disagreement, students debrief and discuss why disagreements can be good. High school students ask the kindergarteners to practice saying, "I beg to differ" and "I respectfully disagree" aloud a few times. The high school students suggest using this language not only during the philosophical discussion but all the time.

Next the high school facilitators explain what philosophy is in simple terms to the kindergarten students. They tell them that studying philosophy means thinking about big ideas and questions that cannot be answered by looking at data, numbers, or evidence. Philosophical questions do not have right or wrong answers.

Kindergarten students are then asked to determine if "Is grass green?" is a philosophical question or not. Students realize the question is not philosophical in nature because you can prove what color grass is. High school facilitators then reiterate that disagreement in philosophy is acceptable and can help everyone in the group learn. Students may change their answers, like facilitators did in the discussion of grass, but you do not have to necessarily do so because there are no right or wrong answers in philosophy.

After the rules of the Game of Philosophy, students read a picture book to the class. Depending on the book, high school students read the book to the whole class at once or break up into two groups. Book such as *The Important Book* and *The Day the Crayons Quit* are read in the smaller group because a discussion is held after each page. Stories such as "Dragons and Giants" from *Frog and Toad Together* and books like *Frederick* are read to the whole class at once because the discussion is held after the story is read straight through.

During the first session, students read *The Important Book* and discuss metaphysics without actually calling it metaphysics. Students debate what makes an apple an apple, what makes a spoon a spoon, and ultimately what makes them the person they are. It is a great introduction to philosophy because students grasp the idea of how to discuss philosophy and they get more invested with each page of the book. It is interesting to hear the diversity of answers for each question. For example, one student felt strongly that it was the flavor that makes an apple an apple, another argued that it was the seeds, while another brought it to a scientific level arguing that it is the molecules.

Using *The Important Book* for the first session enables sophomores to get to know the students that they are working with. Before asking the question "What makes you you?" the high school facilitators go around the circle and have each student say one thing about themselves. The information shared is then used to draw all the children into the conversation about what makes them the person that they are.

Some kindergarten students are shy, so the facilitators do their best to make everyone comfortable. In one room, the facilitators were able to get a shy kindergarten boy who would not say a word during the discussion or anything about himself to open up by noticing he had Spiderman on his sneakers and asking him about it. They asked him if he liked superheroes and were able to bring him out of his shell. The facilitators also open up about themselves to model what they are asking the kindergarten students to do and help create a bond.

During the second session, high school facilitators visited the same classrooms with picture books in hand. After reviewing the rules, the high school students read the kindergarteners a story from the *Frog and Toad* series, "Dragons and Giants." This story centers around what it means to be brave. The questions for this book started with foundational questions, leading up to more abstract questions that students discussed, and ended with the closure question, "What does it mean to be brave?" During the discussion, students' reasons and justifications for supporting an idea move the discussion forward.

What was interesting for us was that in each session there was a mini breakthrough where at least one (or more students) made an insightful contribution that changed the tenor of the discussion and illustrated the evolution of that student's thinking and reasoning within the time we were together. For example, students' definition of bravery became much more expansive, and their perception of this term evolved over the course of the discussion.

This evolution in one's thinking was best exemplified by students' early contributions in which they initially defined bravery as physical strengthen or prowess, yet by the end of our discussion students' perception of bravery evolved, as students were heard saying things such as, "It is brave to run away from danger," and "I think someone is brave when they do anything that they may be scared of doing but they do it anyway." This latter contribution sparked a vibrant discussion of if there are limits to this statement, with some elementary students citing how even what may be a mundane task to many can be frightening to others, and for students who may be afraid of such mundane tasks, by completing them they are brave.

During the discussion, it was difficult but important for us not to provide students with positive or negative feedback, as we did not want to influence future contributions. We furthered the discussion by asking other students what they thought about the previous student's contribution.

High school students provide feedback using a Google form after each philosophy session. Students are asked the following questions:

1. What went well?
2. What issues did you have, if any?
3. Is there anything you would do differently if you had the opportunity to do it over?
4. What was the most memorable comment from a kindergartener?
5. What are you proud of?
6. What is your goal for the next session?
7. Do you have any questions?

Reflection and encouragement are important parts of the process for the facilitators. Students are able to identify areas that need improvement and troubleshoot on their own. They have the freedom to be creative and brainstorm different techniques that might work in their class. Asking students what they are proud of enables students to celebrate their efforts and recognize the great work they are doing. In addition, students feel empowered and confident as they continue on in the process.

Kindergarten teachers also fill out reflection forms after each session. Teachers are asked what went well and what areas can be improved on and are prompted to provide suggestions if they have any. This feedback can be shared with the high school students to help them improve. Collaborating with the kindergarten teachers is valuable since they are experts on their students.

There is noticeable growth in students on both levels from session one to session three. The high school students become more comfortable and confident as countless students have said in their feedback forms. The younger students also become more comfortable with the program and excited for each visit. One kindergarten student said that "philosophy is better than recess!"

IMPACTS OF PHILOSOPHICAL INSTRUCTION

From the start of our foray into philosophy we were determined to empower students to better understand their world through questioning, helping them to become critical consumers of information. In our effort to help students build a foundation for questioning, and not simply accept something because their teacher said it or they read it in book or heard it on the news, we have tapped into students' natural curiosity at this age and provided them with a set of skills or a tool kit in which they can strengthen their metacognitive thinking.

Since introducing philosophical instruction into our practice, we have begun to chart and analyze the impact it has had on students at both the kindergarten and high school levels. While our initial goal was to build a framework for questioning and thinking at the earliest levels of formal schooling, we have found there to be impressive growth in student learning at the high school level as well. While our early data was mostly anecdotal, we have begun the process of formalizing our data collection, and the data we collected thus far is quite promising with specific regards to growth in student writing on state and national exams. Below, we take a brief look at the noticeable changes we have observed in each cohort after their exposure to philosophical instruction.

High School Students

The philosophy program has had a positive impact on student learning in AP World History. The use of evidence-based claims in philosophical discussions has translated to students using more evidence in essays and Socratic seminars. There has also been a marked improvement in students analyzing documents and interpreting point of view. The AP World History exam requires students to write an essay on a Document Based Question (DBQ). After participating in the Big Ideas for Little Kids program, the average score on DBQ essays has increased.

Participation on a daily basis has increased for high school students who have been part of the Big Ideas for Little Kids program. Before running philosophy sessions, many of the students do not see themselves as leaders but afterward they realize their leadership potential. Being a facilitator results in an increase in confidence and an awareness of the value of participating in class. In addition, the training process brings the class together and creates a supportive, collaborative learning environment.

Elementary Students

Although all students have benefited as a result of the program, the most obvious change was in the quiet students in elementary classrooms. Knowing that there are no wrong answers provides students with a sense of freedom and confidence that has helped many students who are usually shy in class join in the conversation. Many teachers have commented that they were surprised by how much their otherwise quiet students talked during the philosophy sessions.

High School and Elementary Students

The Big Ideas for Little Kids program has created a sense of community and provided our youngest learners with great role models both socially and academically. The kindergarten and elementary students viewed the high school students as rock stars to some degree just because they were older. In some classes, the younger students would chant the names of their high school "friends." In many classes, kindergarten students hugged the high school students. One high school student reported being on the receiving end of a running hug at the food store when a kindergarten student recognized him.

The language of respectful discourse is something that students of all ages take away from the program. Kindergarten and elementary teachers have reported that students continue to the use the language of philosophy in class discussions, and in general students speak to each other in a more respectful way after taking part in the program.

One teacher said that she wished her students had participated in the program before the presidential election occurred because she believes it would have provided them with the language to respectfully disagree and listen to opposing viewpoints without feeling personally attacked. One kindergarten student said that he had said "I respectfully disagree" to his mother and, in his words, "My mother almost fell over."

As advancements are made in technology and education evolves, the skills that can be learned from philosophy are more important than ever. We live in an age in which information can be found in a matter of seconds. Students need to have a skill set to know what to do with the information they find. They need to be able to look at sources, ask questions, and make connections between pieces of information to answer big questions. In addition, the interpersonal skills learned during philosophical discussions are more important than ever to learn in school as students are spending more and more of their free time looking at a screen and not interacting with those around them.

EXPANSION OF PROGRAM

With the early success we achieved at the Kindergarten Center, the program has since expanded into grades one through six. After four years of Big Ideas for Little Kids, we have trained over 350 high school students who in turn have become turnkey trainers delivering philosophy lessons to over two thousand kindergarten and elementary students. We have also expanded from our original two to four high school sophomore classes or approximately 120 students each school year who become newly minted philosophical trainers, pushing in to over thirty classrooms every calendar year. While our growth is considerable in a short span of time, we have looked to grow the program organically. We have done this by conducting numerous professional development courses for our elementary teachers.

Our goal is to formalize this process so that in addition to the visits where high school students push into K–6 classrooms, all teachers integrate philosophy into their respective curricula, making it a regular part of their instruction. This will be accomplished via future curriculum writing where we make natural connections between philosophy and existing curricula. This is an important element as we are mindful of the demands of elementary classrooms and state testing, and do not want to frame philosophy as yet another separate requirement for teachers. We view philosophy as a natural enhancement of their existing curriculum.

CONCLUSION

The Big Ideas for Little Kids program does not end for the high school students with the last session at the Kindergarten Center. High school extension lessons have been developed that tie the skills, format, and sometimes even books from the program with history curriculum. For example, students are assigned a group project that asks them to write a page of *The Important Book* on a historical topic. Students work together to brainstorm "important" qualities and details about a historical time period or individual, following the pattern used in *The Important Book* to write and illustrate their page. Students then work together as a group to write a list of questions to have a philosophical discussion based on the page that they created. The project culminates with each group reading their page to the class and leading a discussion on it.

A natural extension of the Big Ideas program was to include parents. The Oceanside School District runs an annual one-day "Parent University" in which workshops are offered on subjects ranging from mental health to healthy eating, and everything in between. The workshop on Big Ideas for Little Kids models how parents can use popular picture books to have meaningful and memorable experiences in reading with their children. After the group of parents participates in a philosophical discussion, they are directed to the Parent section of teachingchildrenphilosophy.org so that they have the tools and book modules to use at home.

In addition, parents are included in the Big Ideas for Little Kids philosophy experience at the Kindergarten Center through the use of optional extension assignments that are sent home after each visit. The handouts inform parents of the book that was read and the philosophical topic covered as well as providing additional activities and follow-up questions that can be done at home. The appendix at the end of this chapter shows a sample of such handouts.

Moving forward, we plan to expand this process through additional professional development for our elementary school teaching staff. We will also continue to have our high school students remain an integral part of this process, working with students in other grade levels as well as in kindergarten. While we believe any parent or teacher can teach philosophy to children through picture books, the true power of Oceanside's program was recognized by putting it in the hands of high school students. Having the ability to interact with children at the other end of the K–12 spectrum is unique and adds an element to this program that strengthens the process of learning at all levels.

Using picture books with five- and six-year-olds, as well as our older elementary students, was the perfect vehicle to introduce philosophy in a natural and familiar manner to students. Philosophy has helped our students build a meaningful framework for thinking and questioning, perhaps something that is needed more than ever in today's society. This philosophical foundation has helped students question the world around them and has strengthened students' overall learning.

APPENDIX 5.1: SAMPLE EXTENSION ASSIGNMENT

Today in school we did Philosophy . . .

AP students from the Oceanside High School visited our class again and practiced **Philosophizing**. We reviewed the **rules of philosophy** and we practiced having a philosophical discussion about bravery. Please discuss with your child what they think bravery is. Ask your child to draw a picture of someone they think is brave and explain why they think that person is brave.

Name:_____

Someone I think is brave is _____.

I think that person is brave because _____
_____

Extension: Thinking like a philosopher allows our children to think deeply and critically at their own unique levels of readiness. It is not about right and wrong answers . . . it is about thinking in different ways. If you think your child is ready to discuss bravery at a deeper level, feel free to use the following questions to facilitate a discussion in your home: Can someone be brave and scared at the same time . . . explain your thinking? Sometimes we think that being scared is a bad thing . . . can being scared be good or helpful in keeping someone safe? If faced with danger, is it better to feel brave or fear . . . why? If you think that someone can be brave and scared at the same time, then what does it mean to be brave?

REFERENCE

Wartenberg, Thomas E. 2009. *Big Ideas for Little Kids: Teaching Philosophy through Children's Literature*. Lanham, MD: Rowman & Littlefield Education.

Chapter Six

The Promise and Challenge of Training College Students as Facilitators

Daniel Groll

For the past three years, the author has offered the course Philosophy with Children, affectionately known as "Phil with Chil," at Carleton College in Northfield, Minnesota. In the course, college students (henceforth just "students") go to Greenvale Park Elementary, an economically and socially diverse[1] school in Northfield, to introduce first and third graders to philosophy through children's literature.[2]

Judging by the interest from the Carleton students, the teachers, and the children, the program has been a success. The students have almost uniformly loved taking the class, with some "alumni" now running their own Philosophy with Children programs in Northfield and beyond. Teachers have been eager to have the program run in their classrooms. Finally, and perhaps most importantly, the children seem to really love the opportunity to talk philosophy and interact with college-age students.

Putting together a Philosophy with Children course is logistically challenging, at least compared to a regular college philosophy class. But it is also, in a way, *conceptually* challenging. It turns out to be more difficult than you might think to accomplish all the goals that should be part of any college-level philosophy class.

In light of these challenges, this paper has two aims. The first is to highlight the tension between (a) preparing college students to effectively do philosophy with children, and (b) offering a course with sufficient rigor to count as a college-level philosophy class. Understanding the nature of this tension is relevant for *anyone* who teaches (at whatever level). The second aim of the paper is to explain, in a way that will be useful to others wanting to start a college Philosophy with Children class, how the program at Carleton College is structured in order to deal with the tension.

WHAT SHOULD A COLLEGE PHILOSOPHY WITH CHILDREN CLASS DO?

The Goals

What would an ideal Philosophy with Children course aim to achieve if the teacher were unconstrained with respect to time and energy? Of course, there is not *one* ideal, but the following six goals are plausible candidates for being part of any Philosophy with Children course:

(1) Engaging children with philosophy
The course aims to engage children with (a) philosophical ideas and (b) methods for thinking about and discussing those ideas, such as asking questions, raising objections, voicing (dis)agreement, offering reasons for their views, and articulating ideas that might seem out of the ordinary or far-fetched.

(2) Teaching students how to engage young children in philosophical discussions/thought
Students must learn how to effectively teach young children philosophy. Most college-level philosophy instruction is not about learning how to teach, but a significant portion of this course must be.

(3) Doing college-level philosophy with the students on the material they will teach
College students should engage, at a college level, with the philosophical material that will figure in the sessions for the children.

(4) Not burdening the teachers at the school
Anyone who has worked with volunteers knows that while they can be absolutely wonderful, they can also sometimes be a managerial burden. One of the central goals of the Carleton program is to ensure this doesn't happen. The hope is that the teacher doesn't need to do anything in the run-up to the sessions or while the students are visiting their classrooms.

(5) Engaging college students with issues in the philosophy of education
There is a vast and fascinating literature on the philosophy of education. (A sample is included in Curren [2007].) Ideally, the students would engage with some of this literature as a way of interrogating not just the aims of the Philosophy with Children course, but also general questions about the nature of education and, more specifically, the proper role of the state in educating its citizens.

(6) Engaging college students with the philosophy behind doing philosophy with children
People have thought long and hard about the nature of philosophizing with children.[3] The students should critically engage with this literature as well.

The first goal is the most important. All the other course goals are subordinate to engaging children with philosophy. How they are subordinate, however, takes a variety of forms.

The value of teaching the students how to teach (goal 2) is more or less entirely explained in terms of its *instrumental* value: It makes the students better at engaging the children with philosophy (goal 1).

However, some of the other goals don't bear much, if any, clear instrumental relationship to engaging children with philosophy. Engaging the students with some literature on the philosophy of education (goal 5) is an independently valuable course goal. Likewise, not burdening the teachers (goal 4) is independently valuable. Its inclusion as a course goal is not explained in terms of how it contributes to engaging the children. Rather, it is worth striving for as a courtesy to the teacher.

The remaining two goals—doing college-level philosophy with the material the students will be teaching (3) and engaging the students with some literature on philosophy with children (6)—are, to borrow from Plato (1992, 357b-d), *mixed* goods. They are not only a means of engaging children with philosophy, but also independently valuable as course goals.

Here's why. Doing college-level philosophy with the material the students will be teaching will make the students better teachers for the simple reason that the experience will give them a deeper understanding of what they are teaching. But it is also worth doing simply as part of a college philosophy class.

Engaging the students with some of the literature on doing philosophy with children will, plausibly, make the students better teachers. But, once again, there is independent reason to have students read some of this literature simply because of the nature of the course.

Combining the Goals

You could, in principle, design a course that achieved all these goals to a satisfying degree. Here is how such a course might go: The students spend two weeks or so reading about the Philosophy for Children movement and the philosophy behind it.[4] Then they might spend two weeks exploring more general issues in the philosophy of education.

Next, they might spend one week, or more, on each of a number of central topics in some of the major subfields of philosophy—epistemology, ethics, political theory, metaphysics, philosophy of language, aesthetics (and the list could go on!)—since they will certainly cover some of these areas in the sessions with the children.

After that, it is time to prepare for the visits to the elementary school: Choosing children's books to workshop, designing and doing presentations on those books, writing up lessons based on the books, preparing the sessions, running through mock sessions, and gathering and preparing activity/craft materials for the sessions. Finally, it is time for the class visits over four weeks.

All told, this course would take approximately twenty weeks, probably more. But if you don't have twenty weeks, you have to make choices. Time constraints put some of the goals in *indirect* tension. But the difficulty of achieving all the goals is not merely the result of limited time. Indeed, some of the goals are in *direct* tension with each other: Achievement of one, by itself, can get in the way of achievement of another.

There is both an indirect and a direct tension between the dominant course goal of engaging children with philosophy and the goal of doing college-level philosophy with the material the students will be teaching. This is somewhat surprising: Doing college-level philosophy with the material they will be teaching is a way of preparing students to engage the children. But then how could the two goals be in direct (or indirect) tension?

Answering this question not only sheds light on the difficulties of putting together a Philosophy with Children course, but also points to a more general lesson about the relationship between two kinds of expertise that anyone who teaches should keep in mind when designing, and teaching, any kind of course.

THE TENSION

To understand the nature of the tension, let's look more closely at how the two goals are *consonant*. If you want students to engage the children, it is helpful—to put it mildly—that the students know the material they are teaching. Doing college-level philosophy with students is likely to make them better at running discussions for the simple reason that being an effective teacher requires that you really understand the material you are teaching. So far, that's common sense.

But it is also common sense that knowing your stuff is not enough to make you an effective teacher. Many, if not all readers, will have been taught by someone who clearly knew his stuff but was, nonetheless, an awful teacher. This means that the students need to learn how to teach in order to bridge the gap between doing college-level philosophy and engaging children with philosophy.

Can the gap be bridged while accomplishing both goals simultaneously? That is: Can the teacher have the students engage with college-level philosophy *through* teaching the students to teach? This is harder to do than it may seem. First, the indirect tension between the two goals runs deeper than it initially appears, and second, there is a *direct* tension between the goals.

Two Kinds of Philosophical Sensitivity

Let's look more closely at the idea that a good teacher knows her stuff. What does that mean? Certainly, a large part of it has to do with understanding the *content* of what you are teaching. The content in a college philosophy session, of course, is going to be very different than that in an elementary school session, even if both sessions are, at some level of description, about the same thing.

For example, both classes might explore the question "What is art?" The college-level class will (should!) talk about Bell's formalism (1927), Dickie's institutional theory of art (2001), and Levinson's intentional-historical theory of art (1979 and 1989) in precisely the terms used by Bell, Dickie, and Levinson.

The elementary school class should not do any of that! Instead, it might involve looking at paintings, sculptures, natural landscapes, and photographs and simply asking, "Is this art? Why? Or why not?" One needn't know anything about philosophical theories of art in order to do that.

Even so, someone doing philosophy with children will benefit from having a fairly firm grasp of the more sophisticated philosophy underlying the comparatively simple content being discussed with the children. Why?

The answer is that grappling with the more sophisticated content is an excellent way of developing what Jana Mohr Lone calls "philosophical sensitivity" (Lone 2012, 23). According to Lone:

> Philosophical sensitivity involves the development of our ability to identify and ponder fundamental questions about the human condition and to be unwilling to stop at whatever answers we find (Lone, 2012, 23).

A key part of having philosophical sensitivity is a willingness and ability to productively interrogate assumptions, experiences, perceptions, beliefs, desires, etc., that might initially seem too obvious to question. As Lone puts it:

> Philosophical sensitivity heightens our awareness that the way things appear to us does not necessarily reflect the way things really are. Development of this capacity allows us to notice the philosophical facets of questions, beliefs, and situations that we might otherwise miss (Lone 2012, 23).

Exercising philosophical sensitivity involves deploying cognitive tools that are especially prominent in philosophy. Philosophical sensitivity "brings together reason and imagination: an ability to utilize logic and analytic capability and the imagination necessary to envision unfamiliar possibilities and find ideas for exploration in the simplest things" (Lone 2012, 23).[5]

Anyone who hopes to teach philosophy—at any level—needs some degree of philosophical sensitivity. One needs to develop a nose for asking questions that advance the discussion, making productive objections, sniffing out hidden assumptions, and offering possible answers that are not immediately apparent.

Having philosophical sensitivity is particularly important when doing philosophy with young children, who have a real predilection for making comments, asking questions, and offering anecdotes that threaten to push discussions wildly off course. It helps tremendously to be able to move nimbly within and across the philosophical terrain you are exploring with the children, so as to steer the discussion back on course.

But the ability to think of a productive question, for example, and the ability to *frame* the question in a way that will engage children are not the same. This is because philosophical sensitivity comes in two varieties: *Inquiry Philosophical Sensitivity* and *Pedagogy Philosophical Sensitivity*.

Inquiry Philosophical Sensitivity is the sensitivity required to shed light on the topic under discussion. The more Inquiry Philosophical Sensitivity you have, the better positioned you are to understand, and indeed contribute, an idea or set of ideas. So, for example, someone with a lot of Inquiry Philosophical Sensitivity with respect to logic is well positioned to understand, and contribute to, ideas in logic. This ability is not just a matter of knowing a lot of logic, but also knowing how to *move*, so to speak, within the domain of logic.

Pedagogy Philosophical Sensitivity is the sensitivity required to convey complicated ideas in a productive way to an audience with less Inquiry Philosophical Sensitivity than the teacher. Having Pedagogy Philosophical Sensitivity involves recognizing where, and why, there are gaps between the teacher's and the audience's level of Inquiry Philosophical Sensitivity. A teacher who tells her students an argument is invalid without realizing that the students have a tenuous grasp on the concept of validity might have lots of Inquiry Philosophical Sensitivity. But she lacks Pedagogy Philosophical Sensitivity, at least in this context.

The crucial thought is this: It is hard to develop Inquiry Philosophical Sensitivity at the very same time as developing Pedagogy Philosophical Sensitivity. This is particularly true if the teacher and audience have very different levels of Inquiry Philosophical Sensitivity.

Of course, developing Pedagogy Philosophical Sensitivity by thinking about how to teach concept X to a particular audience is often an *occasion* for realizing that you don't understand X so well yourself: Every teacher has had the experience of really only learning something for the first time when having to teach it! But when this happens, the teacher needs to go figure things out for himself—he needs to turn to the task of improving his Inquiry Philosophical Sensitivity with respect to X—and *then turn again* to the question of how best to teach the material.

What all this means is that trying to increase students' Inquiry Philosophical Sensitivity through improving their Pedagogy Philosophical Sensitivity (by teaching them how to teach) is none too easy. Students need a chance to grapple with philosophical content *at their own level* in order to inculcate the kind of Inquiry Philosophical Sensitivity that will help them engage children with philosophy. The two steps cannot be so easily combined. And so we end up with the indirect tension between doing college-level philosophy with students and engaging children with philosophy: Time for one means less time for the other.

Moreover, managing the indirect tension is harder than it might first seem. This is because inculcating Inquiry Philosophical Sensitivity takes *time*. While you might be able to get a sense of the major theories of art by reading a few papers or an entry in the *Stanford Encyclopedia of Philosophy*, you will not develop (much) Inquiry Philosophical Sensitivity simply by doing that kind of reading.

Inquiry Philosophical Sensitivity is developed through *doing* philosophy: reading, discussing, writing, wondering, interrogating, objecting, responding, etc. Of course, there is no point at which a person "gets" Inquiry Philosophical Sensitivity after not having it. But giving students even a dose of Inquiry Philosophical Sensitivity requires doing philosophy at a college level over the course of weeks and months.[6] Inasmuch as the instructor does not have weeks and months to devote to doing that, the indirect tension will be difficult to manage.

What about the idea that there is a *direct* tension between the goals of doing college-level philosophy with the students and engaging the children, the idea that achievement of the first by itself tends to get in the way of achievement of the second? Why think that that is true? Here's the basic thought: Inculcating Inquiry Philosophical Sensitivity can make people *less* pedagogically sensitive. Why do you think that is true?

The answer is that as you gain expertise in a field you can easily lose sight of what is common knowledge and what is specialized knowledge. Everyone, no doubt, has had a teacher (or been the teacher) who used a technical term without explanation. The term "normative," for example, is not used much in everyday conversation, so when students first encounter it they generally do not know what it means or how to use it. But the term is used left, right, and center in academic philosophy, so much so that it is very easy for teachers to forget—indeed, to fail to realize in the first place—that it is not a term that students will understand without explanation.

The more Inquiry Philosophical Sensitivity you have, the more terms like "normative"[7] become utterly commonplace, to the point that you can easily lose sight of their oddity and opacity to (relative) outsiders. Teachers often think they are completely clear in making some point only to find out later that the audience got tripped up very early on by invocation of a term the teacher hadn't realized needed explaining.

The greater the gap between the teacher's level of Inquiry Philosophical Sensitivity and the audience's, the more likely the teacher's Inquiry Philosophical Sensitivity will naturally get in the way of her Pedagogy Philosophical Sensitivity. For example, there is almost no gap between the teacher and the audience in a professional talk delivered to one's fellow specialists (indeed, we don't think of the speaker as a teacher in this context). As a result, the teacher needs to give relatively little thought to how she will productively engage her audience.

By way of contrast, philosophy professors know (or should know) that they need to give considerable thought to how to productively engage students. They need to do this precisely because the students typically do not start with anything like the professor's level of Inquiry Philosophical Sensitivity.

How does this relate to doing philosophy with children? There is, obviously, a very large gap between the students' and children's level of Inquiry Philosophical Sensitivity. But perhaps the gap here is so substantial that the need to deal with it is entirely on the surface. The students are aware, straightaway, that they should not use terms like "normativity" with young children! So maybe the direct tension between having Inquiry Philosophical Sensitivity and Pedagogy Philosophical Sensitivity doesn't apply when doing philosophy with children.

Unfortunately, the direct tension is still there for two reasons. First, being aware that you need to present things in a particular way and actually doing it are two different things. If you learned about the nature of justice in a way that uses the term "normative," then you will be inclined to reach for that very term when talking about justice. Unless you have thought about, and planned for, how to talk about it without using the term, you might find yourself gummed up, at a loss.

The second reason the direct tension is present even when doing philosophy with children is this: There are all kinds of *nontechnical* terms that are too sophisticated for children but are so common in philosophical discourse that they are unlikely to come to the attention of teachers who have developed some Inquiry Philosophical Sensitivity (but little Pedagogy Philosophical Sensitivity).

Consider terms like "(im)permissible," "distinction," "authority," "decisive," "objection," and "inference." And now imagine a discussion you might have about Kevin Henke's *Lilly and the Purple Plastic Purse* (2006).

In this story, Lilly's teacher takes her purple plastic purse away because Lilly is misbehaving in class. The book is excellent for thinking about the nature of authority and power. The teacher has the power to take away Lilly's purse. Maybe a fellow classmate (a bigger, stronger classmate!) does too. Does that mean the classmate is allowed to take away the purse? Imagine the classmate wants to take the purse away for exactly the same reason the teacher does. Is there now no difference between the teacher taking away the purse and the classmate doing so?

Someone in a college philosophy class might say something like this:

> There is a distinction between having power and having authority. Just because someone has the power to take away Lilly's purse doesn't mean they have the authority to do so: To infer otherwise would be a mistake. The teacher is permitted to take the purse from Lilly. But another child is not, even if they have the power to take the purse. The teacher's exercise of power is legitimate. The classmate's is not.

Claims like these will get almost no purchase with young children! But the problem is not the presence of *technical* terms—there aren't really any.

The problem, more simply, is that the discourse is too sophisticated. But college students are enculturated into precisely this mode of discourse in college philosophy classes. Someone who has developed some Inquiry Philosophical Sensitivity will naturally talk in this way. In fact, they will find it hard *not* to talk in this way, *even if* they know they should avoid technical terms.

What this means is that developing Inquiry Philosophical Sensitivity in students simultaneously gives them a set of skills that will help them run discussions with children *and* enculturates them into a mode of thinking that must be *overcome* if one hopes to engage children. There is, in other words, a direct tension between doing college-level philosophy with the students and engaging children with philosophy.

THE COURSE

How can a Philosophy with Children course be structured so as to manage the tension (both direct and indirect)? It will not do to run a "regular" philosophy course for most of the term—having students read and write papers—and then send them into the elementary school classroom with minimal planning.

With that in mind, let's begin with an overview of what the sessions at Greenvale Park look like. Assuming that they provide a decent model for engaging children with philosophy, we can ask two questions: (1) What needs to be done to get students to the point where they can run these kinds of sessions? and (2) Where does college-level philosophy fit into the course?

How the Sessions Work

Philosophy with Children enrolls twenty-four students who form four groups of six. Each group visits one classroom (either first or third grade) at Greenvale Park four times in the final four weeks of the ten-week Carleton term. The structure of the sessions is based on the program developed by Thomas Wartenberg at Mount Holyoke College and explained in his book *Big Ideas for Little Kids*. Each session is organized around a children's picture book, which is used as the basis for discussing a set of topics.

The hour-long sessions always begin with the student leaders reading the story (approximately ten minutes).[8] The class is then broken into two groups, with the student leaders each taking charge of one group. The remaining students distribute themselves between the two groups. Discussion begins with a story matrix. As Wartenberg explains:

> The story matrix takes the book's narrative—a series of events that unfolds sequentially in time, generally speaking—and puts them into a logical structure involving fundamental categories that the children will have to use in order to have a philosophy discussion (Wartenberg 2014, 49).

The matrix is constructed on a large sheet of flip-board paper. It contains questions that simultaneously jog the children's memory about the main elements in the story and focus their thoughts on topics for the discussion to come. It "creates a visual record of the interpreted story that [the instructors] and the children can continue to refer to during the discussion." (Wartenberg 2014, 49–50).[9] After the group completes the matrix (about ten minutes), they have a roughly twenty-five-minute discussion. The sessions end with an activity that, ideally, provides a hands-on instantiation of some of the discussion topics.

Let's look at an example of a successful session that was built around the story *The Dot* by Peter Reynolds (2003). In the story, a young girl named Vashti is convinced that she can't draw. Her teacher encourages her to "make a mark and see where it takes you." Vashti makes a mark on the page in frustration. Her teacher asks her to sign it. The next week, Vashti is surprised to find her dot displayed in a frame for everyone to see. Realizing she can draw a better dot, Vashti begins creating many more dots, in all different colors, sizes, and styles. An artist is born![10]

The story provides a fabulous starting point for a discussion about the nature and value of art. It also allows for very easy use of visual prompts that keep young children engaged. For example, the students showed the children pictures of various artworks across different mediums and asked whether the works in question are art.[11] Nascent theories of art were articulated. Many children claimed that photographs are never art. Others claimed that anything painted is art. After the discussion, the children were given pre-"framed" pieces of paper, bottle caps, feathers, and other sundry materials and encouraged to make their own unconventional art.

The content and structure of the session are not particularly surprising. Nor is there any great mystery, considered at a high-enough level of generality, about what needed to happen to prepare the students to run the session. They needed to identify *The Dot* as a good candidate for a session; they needed to learn something about the philosophy of art; they needed to figure out their discussion questions; and they needed to design an activity.

But this brief summary belies the difficulty of running really strong sessions. You can run perfectly mediocre sessions without much effort. Reading a story, constructing a story matrix,[12] and cobbling together a discussion about what makes something art isn't particularly demanding. Putting together an activity takes some work, but not much if the activity is something as simple as drawing a picture.

However, it takes a lot of planning and practice to run really good sessions. In a really good session the story is read with genuine feeling; the story matrix is constructed to elicit responses that will be used in the subsequent discussion; the discussion questions are formulated and scaffolded in a way that gets kids talking and moves the discussion from a very simple starting point (e.g., "Do you think X's picture was art? Let's take a vote!") to a more complex ending point (e.g., "So, why do we call things that are so different from each other—music, dance, sculpture, etc.,—art?"); the activity is connected to the philosophical content of the discussion.

All of that is about making the *content* really good. But running a good session involves more than having great content. As we have seen, the students must have sufficient philosophical sensitivity—both Inquiry and Pedagogy—to effectively steer discussion.

In addition, they must think seriously about classroom management. For example: How should the children and college students arrange themselves during the story? What is the plan for splitting up the children into groups for discussion? Where will the two groups be in the classroom? Do the story matrices need to be taped to the wall? Who will do that? Do some children need a little more guidance in order to stay focused? Which students will provide that guidance? Should a student make a special point to sit between two children who tend to distract each other? Who will that be? What supplies are required for the activity and who will bring them?

Of course, issues like these can be worked out on the fly. But the students should work out as many of them as possible before heading into the classroom, for three reasons. First, students often will not have thought about some classroom management issues *at all*, so they may not even notice that there's something that should be dealt with. For example, students tend not to think about where they should sit in order to effectively manage the group of children they're dealing with.

Second, working things out on the fly eats up precious time. Suppose the students have not planned where the discussion groups will go after the story. As a result, desks have not been pushed to the side to create room. So now the students must consult each other—and the classroom teacher if she is there—and push the desks out of the way. This is not a huge deal. But it still takes time away from what matters. Indeed, substantial time may be lost when there are multiple interruptions of this sort.

Finally, and most importantly, working things out on the fly creates "gaps" during the session where the students are not focused on the children. These gaps can kill the session's momentum. They also make it more likely that the students will—even if only briefly—lose control of the session as unengaged children start to get antsy or bored. Managing young children is hard enough when there is actually something for the children to do. It is much harder to manage them when they have nothing to do (even if only briefly)!

So, planning really good sessions takes serious time. It takes time to make the content strong. And it takes time to work out the *flow* of the session so as to minimize the number of "gaps."

With all that in mind, we can turn to the question of how to prepare the students to succeed in the sessions. What needs to happen in the weeks leading up to the sessions to ensure as much as possible that the sessions are excellent?

Preparing the Students to Enter the Classroom

Developing the content for a successful session and working out the classroom management details takes *practice*. Students need to practice reading out loud, putting together and presenting a story matrix, running a discussion, and running an activity. They get lots of practice while actually running the sessions: As the weeks go on, the sessions tend to get better as the students learn from their mistakes (and get to know the children).

However, in order to offer engaging sessions from the start, and to adhere to the goal of not burdening the teacher, a good portion of the practicing—and the trying and failing that come with it—must happen *before* the students head to Greenvale Park. The bulk of the course prior to the sessions, then, is devoted to giving the students a chance to practice. Here's how that is done.

The first course session is devoted to explaining the course logistics, and then watching and discussing the WGBY documentary *Big Ideas for Little Kids* (Akeret 2014). Students are assigned to read a significant portion of Wartenberg's book for the second session. Central parts of the book are discussed, along with ideas on how to use children's literature to foster philosophical discussion and how to build a story matrix. The students collaboratively construct a running list of points from the book that are particularly worth remembering for when *they* start planning and executing lessons.

In the second half of that session, the instructor reads and presents a children's book in order to provide a model of what the students' presentation should look like. The next three weeks are devoted to those student presentations. Student pairs each choose two children's books to use as the basis for presentations to half the class.[13] After reading the book out loud to their peers (usually poorly the first time around), the students run a forty-five-minute *college-level* discussion on the philosophical themes in the book.

The students prepare for this discussion by reading a couple of papers and, perhaps, the *Stanford Encyclopedia of Philosophy* entry (or entries) on the topics they plan to discuss. The final fifteen minutes of the session are devoted to talking about how the college-level questions might be made into first- or third-grade-level questions.

The students write a book module (Wartenberg 2014, 165) based on the presentation and feedback from the instructor or TA.[14] The book modules are a distillation of the presentation and, crucially, the students' first pass at carefully presenting the ideas in their chosen book at something less than a college level. This "leveling-down" happens in two places.

First, the module has a philosophical overview, which is intended for a teacher—or indeed anyone who wants to do philosophy with children—to gain a quick grasp of the issues and themes. Since the audience for this part of the module is someone who has never done academic philosophy the overview must be written for an interested lay audience. So, terms or formulations that the students used in their presentation might need to be substantially reformulated.

The second, more substantial leveling down happens in the second part of the module where students must formulate the questions one might actually use in a discussion with children. Lots of thought must be given to how to formulate these questions, in order to get the children talking.

After all the presentations, students are divided into four groups of six (one group for each classroom at Greenvale Park). Each group decides which four books they would like to use for their sessions. Crucially, they are not required to use the books they presented. The guiding question when choosing books for the sessions is, simply: "What will make for a good session with the children?" Having settled on their four books, the group divides into pairs, each choosing one book as the basis for their session.[15] The pairs spend the coming weeks preparing for their sessions, including figuring out, and tracking down, what supplies they need.[16]

The visits to the school take place in the second course session of the week. The first course session is devoted to a run-through of that week's entire session: The leaders read the story, run through a story matrix, lead a discussion with their peers (who are now instructed to act, as best they can, like first or third graders), and run the activity.

The run-through is crucial for now familiar reasons: Students often realize that their story matrix doesn't work quite the way they thought it would; or that some line of questioning might lead in a direction they had not anticipated at all; or that some aspect of their activity has not been thought through well enough ("What's your plan for attaching *this* to *that*?"). The run-throughs for the first session invariably make clear to the students the difference between being *kind of /more or less prepared* and being *really and truly prepared*. Stern words from the instructor on the difference usually ensures that future groups are really and truly prepared!

The four groups (one for each class at Greenvale Park) run their mock sessions simultaneously. The instructor and the TA do the rounds to check on the mock sessions, answer questions, and make suggestions. Student leaders are required to upload a detailed lesson plan to the course website the next day, and all members of the group are required to familiarize themselves with it. At this point, the students are ready to run their session.

MANAGING THE TENSION

One can see from the above description that the course is almost entirely devoted to preparing the students to engage children with philosophy. Students are neither assigned, nor taught, "straight" philosophy readings of any kind. Nor are they required to write a standard philosophy paper. How, then, is the goal of engaging the students with college-level philosophy, and so developing their Inquiry Philosophical Sensitivity, incorporated into the class?

One answer is that they don't need to develop Inquiry Philosophical Sensitivity in *this* particular class. Instead, the instructor might design the course so that the students come into it with a fair amount of Inquiry Philosophical Sensitivity. So, for example, the instructor might have a strong prerequisite requirement: Perhaps students need to each have taken two prior philosophy courses or be a philosophy major.

In addition, the instructor could encourage, if not require, students to choose topics for their lessons that they already know something about. The students will then already be fairly well positioned to engage children because they (the students) will already have some Inquiry Philosophical Sensitivity with respect to what they are teaching. The Philosophy with Children course can then focus on developing the students' Pedagogy Philosophical Sensitivity.

The problem with this approach is that if the students are not required to engage with novel topics, then the course has effectively abandoned the goal of engaging students with college-level philosophy. Depending on institutional norms, offering such a course could be a possibility. But it shouldn't obviously bill itself as a college-level philosophy class worth full credit.

Perhaps the instructor could require students to choose topics that cover areas of philosophy they are unfamiliar with but still limit the course to students who have taken a decent amount of philosophy. The students would come into the class with a fair degree of Inquiry Philosophical Sensitivity and so be more likely to absorb the contours of the new topics by doing independent research for their presentations. One might also require that the students write standard philosophy papers on the topics of their book.

This option arguably does the best of managing the tension between doing college-level philosophy with the students and engaging children with philosophy. But it is not a viable option at schools with a small student body. There is no hope of filling the Philosophy with Children course at Carleton with only philosophy majors or students who have taken multiple philosophy courses.

What about dropping the prerequisite altogether? The problem is that it is not productive to have students who have *never* taken a philosophy course do their own research to prepare for their presentations. It is also arguably unfair to have those students write standard papers on topics that have not been explicitly covered by the professor in class.

The Carleton College course tries to stake out a middle ground between these options. There is a prerequisite of one prior philosophy course, which ensures that the students in the course have read and written some philosophy. Students can choose whatever books and topics they want.

Most choose books that explore topics they are interested in but not hugely familiar with. In the course of preparing their presentations—and often in consultation with the instructor—students discover that their book invites discussion of more philosophical topics than they thought. They learn something about those topics in preparing for their presentations to their peers and (to a lesser extent) listening to (and asking questions during) other people's presentations. They also must distill what they have learned into the first section of their book modules, which provides a philosophical overview of the book.

All in all, then, the Carleton College course substantially subordinates the goal of doing college-level philosophy to the goal of engaging children with philosophy. Given the need to inculcate Pedagogy Philosophical Sensitivity through practice, there is not enough time to engage with college-level philosophy content outside of the context of the students presenting their books and then writing book modules.

One consequence of this approach to managing the tension between engaging children with philosophy and doing college-level philosophy with the students is that the Carleton College course does not automatically count toward completing the major. If a student wants it to count, she must write a seven-to-ten-page philosophy paper on one of the topics she covered over the course of the term. The alternative to writing a paper—and the one that most students choose—is to produce their own children's book with an accompanying book module.

Why not have everyone write a term paper? We have already seen the answer: Requiring students to write substantial papers on topics that have not been explicitly discussed, debated, and explained in class is unfair. This is because very little of what happens in class is geared toward giving students the depth of understanding—of either philosophical content or methodology—to write a strong term paper.

CONCLUSION: PUTTING THE COURSE IN CONTEXT

So where does that leave someone who is thinking about putting together a Philosophy with Children class? Is it an appropriate class to offer at the college level? Once the course is seen in the right context, the answer is a resounding "yes."

First, the Philosophy with Children course is the only nontraditional philosophy course at Carleton College. Moreover, given the prerequisite for the course, Philosophy with Children won't be a student's only exposure to philosophy. Indeed, some students take a normal philosophy course so that they can meet the prerequisite to take Philosophy with Children. So, while the course itself might not be everything a college philosophy course should be, it can be part of a program that sees students studying *more* philosophy than they otherwise might.

The second important bit of context is this: Since its inception, ten "alumni" of the course have developed their own Philosophy with Children programs. Two of these programs were afterschool programs at Greenvale Park. Perhaps more impressively, three former students have developed programs of their own in Michigan, Georgia, and China. The course, then, likely does more than a typical college philosophy class to create opportunities for people—some of the students that take the course, the children at Greenvale Park, and the children that work with a spin-off program—to do philosophy. Focusing only on whether Philosophy with Children does enough college-level philosophy is, perhaps, missing the forest for the trees.[17]

The upshot is that despite the challenges articulated in this chapter, the course at Carleton does indeed provide a good model for doing philosophy with children with college students. It may not do everything that one would want a philosophy course to do. But then, what course does? As part of an overall philosophy curriculum, a Philosophy with Children course not only gives students a valuable opportunity to apply their knowledge outside the classroom but creates opportunities for doing philosophy that traditional courses do not.

NOTES

1. At least by the standards of Northfield, Minnesota. The Greenvale Park student body is about 26 percent Latino. Forty-two percent of all students are on the free or reduced lunch program. Eighteen percent are English language learners.

2. The program follows the model pioneered by Thomas Wartenberg at Mt Holyoke College and explained in his 2014 book, *Big Ideas for Little Kids: Teaching Philosophy through Children's Literature.*

3. For a good sample of what is available, see www.plato-philosophy.org/resourcetypes/books/

4. For an overview see Michael Pritchard (2018).

5. Clearly this notion of philosophical sensitivity is closely related to the goal of engaging the children with philosophy articulated above. Indeed, we might understand that goal largely in terms of developing philosophical sensitivity in the students.

6. Or, so as not to be too parochial about it, some form of humanistic inquiry.

7. Other examples might include terms like "affirming the consequent," "validity," "deontology," "categorical," "all things considered," "prudential," "*pro tanto*."

8. The first session is an exception: It begins by briefly talking about what philosophy is and our rules for doing philosophy. This, too, follows Wartenberg's model. See Wartenberg 2014, 44.

9. See Wartenberg 2014, page 50, for an example.

10. This synopsis of the book is, with a few modifications, taken from the book module for *The Dot* written by two students from the Carleton Philosophy with Children course, Daniel Gorter and Sarah Magid. You can see the whole module at: www.teachingchildrenphilosophy.org/BookModule/TheDot.

11. Duchamp's urinal was a big hit.

12. Actually two, since the class is split into two for discussion.

13. In order to get through all the presentations (remember, each pair does two), the course requires a teaching assistant who oversees one of the presentations by each pair. While the TA provides feedback, she does not grade the presentation. The instructor grades the presentation done in front of him. So, each pair has one of their presentations graded.

14. See teachingchildrenphilosophy.org for many, many book modules, including a good number done by students from Carleton College.

15. Since there are only six people in each group, two people must volunteer to run an additional session. Why six people in each group rather than eight? An iteration of the course with thirty-two people proved to be too logistically daunting. There was no "breathing room" in the course structure to accommodate problems when they (inevitably) arose, e.g., someone falling ill and so not being able to present.

16. Who pays for these supplies? And what about the children's books—where do they come from? The course at Carleton has been generously supported by grants from the Puzak Fund as well as the Carleton College Center for Community and Civic Engagement, which allowed us to buy all the books (we give them to Greenvale Park at the end of the term) and supplies.

17. Many thanks to Thomas Wartenberg for comments on an earlier draft as well as Dorothy MacKinnon for being an excellent editor.

REFERENCES

Akeret, Julie. 2014. *Big Ideas for Little Kids: Teaching Philosophy through Picture Books.* Wgby.org/bigideas.

Bell, Clive. 1927. *Art*. London: Capricorn Books, 15–35.

Curren, Randall, ed. 2007. *The Philosophy of Education: An Anthology.* Malden, MA: Wiley-Blackwell.

Dickie, George. 2001. *Art and Value*. Malden, MA: Wiley-Blackwell.

Henkes, Kevin. 2006. *Lilly's Purple Plastic Purse*. New York: Greenwillow Books.

Levinson, Jerrold. 1979. "Defining Art Historically." *British Journal of Aesthetics* 19, no. 3: 232–50.

Levinson, Jerrold. 1989. "Refining Art Historically." *Journal of Aesthetics and Art Criticism* 47, no. 1: 21–33.

Lone, Jana Mohr. 2012. *The Philosophical Child*. Lanham, MD: Rowman & Littlefield.

Plato. *Republic*. 1982. Translated by G. M. A. Grube. Indianapolis, IN: Hackett.

Pritchard, Michael. 2018. "Philosophy for Children." In *The Stanford Encyclopedia of Philosophy*. https://plato.stanford.edu/entries/children/.

Randall Curren, ed. 2007. *The Philosophy of Education: An Anthology.* Malden, MA: Wiley-Blackwell.

Reynolds, Peter Hamilton, Thora Birch, and Jerry Dale McFadden. 2003. *The Dot*. Nottingham, UK: Candlewick Press.

Wartenberg, Thomas E. 2014. *Big Ideas for Little Kids: Teaching Philosophy through Children's Literature. 2nd edition*. Lanham, MD: Rowman & Littlefield.

Chapter Seven

Picture Books Go to College

Introducing Philosophy to Undergraduates[1]

Thomas E. Wartenberg

Working with elementary school children had a major impact on my teaching at the college level. In this chapter, I describe an introduction to philosophy course based upon picture books developed for first-year undergraduate students at Mount Holyoke College.

Only as a result of seeing how effectively picture books fostered philosophical discussions among young children did the idea for this course even occur to me. It serves as an example of the reciprocal influence of teaching philosophy at the college and elementary school levels, a relationship that has not been adequately explored.

PICTURE BOOKS AS PROMPTS FOR PHILOSOPHY DISCUSSIONS

As the previous chapters in this anthology have made clear, picture books are a very effective means for initiating philosophy discussions among young children. Children love picture books and, in particular, having them read to them by adults. In fact, being read to is the single most important factor in children becoming lifelong readers (Trelease 2013, 4). Having had picture books read to them clearly has a major effect upon children's lives.

It's easy to get children excited about having a philosophical discussion about philosophical issues they have encountered in a picture book. Although it may take some effort to manage the discussions that result, children love taking part in freewheeling discussions of such issues as: "Do we have free will or are all of our actions determined by some factor over which we have no control, like our biology?" and "Are dreams less real than our normal waking reality?"

The elementary school philosophy course described in my book *Big Ideas for Little Kids: Teaching Philosophy through Children's Literature* has been taught for nearly two decades in schools in western Massachusetts. It began with the college students going into the Jackson Street School in Northampton. For the past twelve years, the college students have taught philosophy at the Martin Luther King Jr. Charter School of Excellence in Springfield. The elementary school course was modeled on the structure of the type of introduction to philosophy course that is often offered to undergraduate students in the United States.

A basic feature of this elementary school philosophy course is that it covers a range of different philosophical issues drawn from the major fields of philosophy: certainly, ethics and social and political philosophy, but also epistemology (the theory of knowledge), metaphysics (the nature of reality), philosophy of mind, and aesthetics (including the philosophy of art). You can find many examples of books that fit these categories at https://www.teachingchildrenphilosophy.org/Category, the website that was developed as part of the Philosophy for Children course at Mount Holyoke.

Given that the model for the elementary school philosophy course was an undergraduate introduction to philosophy, it is somewhat surprising that for many years I did not consider transferring aspects of the elementary school philosophy course back into a college-level introduction to philosophy course. Eventually, I did so and developed an introduction to philosophy course that used picture books as a central element.

The occasion for the development of this course was a requirement instituted by Mount Holyoke College that every faculty member teach an introductory seminar exclusively for first-year students. Faced with the task of developing and teaching such a seminar, rather than just adapting the introductory course I had taught many times before, it seemed worth trying an experiment and seeing what would happen if the introduction to philosophy seminar for first-year students had picture books playing a central role.

The course was taught for the first time in the fall of 2010 and proved to be an unqualified success, although there were elements of the course that required some fine-tuning. The first-year students, all of whom were women, Mount Holyoke being a women's college, loved listening to me reading them the picture books, perhaps in part because I always did so using voices to distinguish the different characters. What is more entertaining to a student in their first semester of college than seeing their philosophy professor attempting to sound like a toad and then use a different voice to impersonate a frog?

Although it was not done intentionally, the course embodies the central features that Ken Bain (2004, 108–9) identified as central to successful teaching: (1) The problems the students attempt to solve are ones they find intriguing;

(2) Their attempts take place in a challenging but supportive environment; (3) They work collaboratively with their peers; and (4) They get feedback about their efforts from their peers before receiving official evaluation of it.

The balance of this chapter explains how the course embodies these goals by describing the structure of the picture-book introduction to philosophy course for first-year students. In addition, the chapter includes an assessment of the course, with both positive and negative outcomes included.

A PICTURE-BOOK INTRODUCTION TO PHILOSOPHY COURSE FOR UNDERGRADUATES

The introduction to philosophy course consists of six units. Each unit begins with a picture book. The professor reads the book aloud to the students and then, following the model employed with elementary school children, asks the students a question that focuses on one philosophical issue that the book raises.

The story that begins the first unit of the course—the topic of the unit is willpower—is "Cookies" from Arnold Lobel's classic book *Frog and Toad Together*. The story is quite funny, as Frog and Toad try not to get sick because they can't resist eating that very last cookie which will be the one that makes them sick!

"Cookies" raises the question of whether the concept of willpower is coherent. After Frog tells Toad that they need more willpower, Toad is puzzled because he doesn't know what willpower is. Frog explains that willpower is "trying hard not to do what you really want to do," in effect proposing a definition of the concept.

Frog's definition is puzzling. After all, if you really want to do something, there is no reason *not* to just go ahead and do it. Why would you try not to do something you really want to do? Should we reject the concept of willpower as incoherent? Or does it play an important role in thinking about why we have trouble with following through on our desires? Clearly, a philosophical discussion is needed to make sense of this concept and the phenomena it attempts to conceptualize.

The discussion the first-year college students engaged in was guided by the ideal of a community of inquiry, a concept discussed briefly in the introduction and a number of the chapters of this anthology. The fundamental idea of a community of inquiry is for students to investigate an issue through interacting with one another, with the teacher functioning solely as a facilitator, a moderator of the discussion. What's essential to the community of inquiry is that the teacher only intervene to move the discussion along and not make substantive contributions of her own.

Jumping into a discussion of Frog's attempt to define willpower would be difficult for first-year students with no philosophical background. So, to get the discussion going in a positive direction, the question that begins the inquiry is whether either, both, or neither Frog or Toad has willpower at the end of the story.

This question makes sense because, after all his efforts to keep from eating more cookies are foiled by Toad, Frog gives the remaining cookies away to a flock of birds. His hope is that this will keep him and Toad from eating so many cookies that they get sick to their stomach. Ever the skeptic, the frustrated and somewhat shortsighted Toad stomps off to bake a cake, telling Frog that he can keep his vaunted willpower.

The ensuing discussion was vibrant. The college students disagreed vehemently about whether Frog and Toad had willpower. Some said that neither could have willpower at the end of the story since there were no cookies left to provide the opportunity to exhibit it. Others thought Frog did have willpower since he had done what was necessary to keep Toad and himself from getting sick as a result of eating too many cookies. Opinions about Toad were also varied, though the majority thought he clearly lacked willpower since he was always trying to find ways to get at the cookies that Frog had attempted to make inaccessible.

The students' first assignment is to write a short paper of no more than two pages in which they state whether they think Frog and Toad had willpower at the end of the story and supply reasons to support their answers that involve explaining whether they agree with Frog's definition of willpower.

Their papers become the subject for the next class session during which the students critique one another's papers. This idea came from a Philosophy and Practice of Art class I had taught with Rie Hachiyanagi, a studio art professor at Mount Holyoke College.

As part of that class, the students had to produce artworks and then critique one another's work. The care with which the students assessed their classmates' work and the critical skills they brought to bear in so doing were impressive and quite surprising. The students showed no hesitation in making serious criticisms of their peers' work. I came away wondering whether philosophy students would be able to exercise the same level of critical engagement with their classmates' work.

For the critique session in the introduction to philosophy class, the students are divided into groups of three and four. Each student brings enough copies of their papers for everyone to have one. Each student's paper becomes the focus for the group in turn.

The student whose turn it is passes out the papers to her peers, who spend about ten minutes reading it and making notes. The student then reads the paper out loud, giving her the opportunity to see more clearly any shortcomings it may have had. There is then a fifteen-minute discussion in which the other students in the small group shared their reactions to the paper, mentioning what they find positive in it but also discussing their criticisms.

The reading for the next class session is a philosophical work chosen because of its focus on the same topic that the students had written about. One reason "Cookies" was such a good place to begin the course is that two Australian philosophers, Jeanette Kennett and Michael Smith, published an essay attempting to defend Frog's definition of willpower, "Frog and Toad Lose Control" (1996). It is a good example of a work of professional philosophy despite its being inspired by a children's picture book and the claims made within it.

Having the college students read a standard philosophical work is a major departure from the structure of the elementary school philosophy course. Although discussing and writing about a picture book allows the college students to formulate their own ideas about a philosophical topic without being intimidated or influenced by having read what philosophers said about it, that is only the first step in learning how to philosophize.

Philosophy is a complex practice with many different aspects to it. The picture-book introduction to philosophy class provides a set of exercises that help the college students develop a range of important skills that are necessary for doing philosophy. These skills build on one another and are all necessary for a student to become proficient at the "game" of philosophy.

The crucial philosophical skills that reading articles by professional philosophers helps them learn are how to read, understand, and criticize a view developed by the authors. The students already began developing their ability to understand an argument and criticize it through reading their classmates' papers. Applying those skills to a more complex and difficult piece of writing was a natural way to develop and hone those skills.

So, in the following class session the students begin by unpacking the argument put forward by the authors they had read. In the case of "Frog and Toad Lose Control," there is a lot of philosophical terminology that needs to be explored, for Kennett and Smith develop a series of distinctions in order to be able to endorse Frog's definition of willpower and claim to have willpower at the end of the story.

For example, they argue that willpower can be exercised either "synchronically" or "diachronically." In the former case, an action is performed that allows one to simultaneously exercise willpower. An example is Frog's putting the cookies on top of a cabinet so that neither he or Toad can reach them, a strategy that Toad immediately figures out how to outwit.

To exercise willpower diachronically, one does something at a certain point in time in order that one not succumb to one's desires at a later time.

Frog's giving the cookies to the birds is an example of this, for it allows him not to eat the fatal last cookie, something he would have done had there been more cookies left.

Working through this and other distinctions elaborated by Kennett and Smith let the undergraduates see that a great deal of philosophical theorizing is necessary in order to defend the claims made in "Cookies." Although many of them were initially skeptical of Frog's claim to have a lot of willpower at the end of the story, they were fascinated by the way in which Kennett and Smith defended Frog's claim.

Because their papers included their own assessments of the validity of Frog's definition of willpower, they want to understand how Kennett and Smith defend Frog's claim (and the book's) that he had willpower at the end of the story. They thus had already developed an initial understanding of the problems surrounding "willpower," so that they are more easily able to comprehend the difficult philosophical distinctions Kennett and Smith developed.

Puzzling through Kennett and Smith's argument also results in even the most skeptical student coming to accept the notion that a picture book could have "serious" philosophical content. For all its charm and humor, "Cookies" raises an issue that philosophers have expended a great deal of effort in resolving, namely, how one can know what the right thing to do is and yet choose not to do it.

The problem of "weakness of the will" is one of the old chestnuts that philosophers and their students still break their teeth chewing on. Discovering what precisely the issue concerning weakness of the will is through contemplating a children's story enables students to have a more solid grasp of it than first encountering it in a difficult philosophical text they have to struggle to understand.

Having discussed Kennett and Smith's article, the students are asked to rewrite their original papers incorporating a discussion of the article. The goal is to have them take their own philosophical views and develop them in a more nuanced manner through a critical engagement with Kennett and Smith's essay.

So, if they had denied that Frog had willpower at the end of the story, for example, they would have to include a response to Kennett and Smith's claim that he did have diachronic willpower. This conceptual refinement of the notion of willpower is just one example of what the students now had to think about in presenting their conclusions.

The following class consists of another critique session, only this time the students work in pairs. Given that their essays were now longer, this is necessary given the brevity of the class periods. This second critique session is quite important, for it provides the students with the feedback they need before revising their papers once more. It was this paper that they handed in for the final grade for this unit of the course.

Too often, students write papers for their courses at the last minute with a deadline looming. This conveys the impression that writing is something that you do when faced with a deadline. But professional writers know that "all writing is rewriting," a motto that is repeated often in this course. The course is structured so that students would have rewritten their initial essays twice before submitting something that was considered their final paper, provisional as that designation really is.

Although the students are graded on each step in the process, their final papers count most heavily toward their final grade. The justification for this is that this paper is the outcome of a two-week process and shows most clearly what they had learned, both in terms of content—what willpower really is—and form—how to analyze and defend a philosophical position.

You'll recall that each of the course's six units begins with a picture book. "Cookies" is only a twelve-page story, many of whose pages are nearly completely taken up with Lobel's charming illustrations. On such a "thin" basis, a two-week unit of the course is structured that allows students to not only develop their own ideas, but to test those ideas out against the views of some professional philosophers and the responses of their peers.

The picture-book introduction to philosophy course consists of six two-week units that have a similar structure. Each is organized around a philosophical question that a picture book raises. Table 7.1 summarizes the philosophical topic addressed in each unit and the readings assigned.

Table 7.1. The Units of the Picture-Book Philosophy Course for First-Year College Students

Philosophical Field	Picture Book	Reading by a Professional Philosopher
Unit 1: Ethics: What is willpower?	"Cookies" by Arnold Lobel	Kennett and Smith, "Frog and Toad Lose Control"
Unit 2: Epistemology: Can we be certain that some of our beliefs are true?	*Many Moons* by James Thurber	Moore, "A Defense of Common Sense"
Unit 3: Social and Political Philosophy: What is the nature of racism?	*The Sneetches* by Dr. Seuss	Goldberg, "Racism and Rationality"
Unit 4: Metaphysics: Can you do nothing?	*Let's Do Nothing* by Tony Fucille	Sartre, "The Origin of Negation"
Unit 5: Aesthetics: Is perfection attainable?	*Ish* by Peter H. Reynolds	Tsanoff, "The Notion of Perfection"
Unit 6: Philosophy of Mind: What is the relationship between real things and imaginary ones?	*Harold and the Purple Crayon* by Crockett Johnson	Nichols, "Imagination and Immortality"

As you can see from this chart, the course uses picture books to introduce philosophical questions drawn from the central areas of philosophy. Any college-level introduction to philosophy class would include a similar diversity of philosophical fields that students would be introduced to.

ASSESSMENT OF THE COURSE

As mentioned earlier, the picture-book introduction to philosophy class is a definite success. Nonetheless, some significant problems emerged as well. Both of these will now be addressed.

Beginning each unit of the course with a picture book turns out to be a great idea. It provides a means for incorporating into a college class one central Big Idea from the elementary school class: that philosophy is best learned when students formulate their own ideas and test them out on each other. This is a departure from how many college and university professors conduct their own classrooms.

In my own history of philosophy classes, for example, classes often involve my explaining a difficult text to the students who can raise questions but who don't get to say what they think about, say, whether it is possible to doubt all of your beliefs, a claim central to Descartes's first *Meditation*. But in the picture-book philosophy course, students begin by articulating the philosophical problem they see the picture book raising and what they think about it.

Their classmates then weigh in with their own reactions and ideas, with the professor only intervening to keep the discussion on track by, for example, focusing it on a comment made by one of the students: "Mathilda just raised an interesting point, that doubts occur in our everyday experience when something goes awry. Do you agree with her?"

A high school philosophy teacher who had read my book *A Sneetch Is a Sneetch and Other Philosophical Discoveries* (2013) decided to incorporate picture books into the epistemology course that he had been teaching for years. Steve Goldberg reported that beginning a unit of the course with a picture book resulted in his students having a deeper and more thoughtful engagement with the materials he taught in the unit.

Goldberg's experience in his course confirms my own: Having students engage with a philosophical issue by introducing it with a picture book results in a more lively and insightful discussion.

Sometimes those discussions develop in an unanticipated direction. For example, I had assumed that *Many Moons* would introduce the question of the relativity of our knowledge since all of the king's experts and his daughter have different ideas about the size of the moon and its distance from us.

But the students wound up talking about certainty, the question of whether there are certain beliefs that you could justifiably claim to be immune from doubt. So my plans to have them read an article about epistemological relativism had to be scrapped in favor of an article about certainty.

The students thus read G. E. Moore's "A Defense of Common Sense." Fortunately, I had told the students that I would choose the paper to assign in each unit only after having heard their discussions, so this did not necessitate me having to explain to them that I was changing the reading. I just placed Moore's essay online for them to read and the course proceeded.

The most challenging aspect of the course is the writing and critique sessions. First, the writing assignments.

The students sometimes became frustrated about the writing and rewriting. As mentioned earlier, requiring students to rewrite an assignment twice before handing it in is a central feature of the course, one that is especially important for beginning college students.[2] The intention behind this double rewrite is getting the students to learn to rewrite papers before handing them in because the process of writing and rewriting allows one to present one's ideas more clearly and forcefully.

The problem is that students in the course sometimes found the incorporation of the scholarly article into their initial articles difficult to manage. Admittedly, this particular type of "rewrite" is something they likely would only be required to do in this course, since few if any other courses would ask them to develop an initial draft without having read the scholarly material they eventually would incorporate into their essays.

The main problem is that there was not always a good fit between where they began and what they had to incorporate into their essay. Exercising great care in choosing the reading to fit their initial papers helps a great deal, as when the Moore essay was assigned in place of one on relativism.

A subsidiary issue has to do with the difficulty of the texts they had to read. Admittedly, Sartre's discussion of nothingness is extremely difficult, to say the least. So it was hard for them to know how to incorporate Sartre's paradoxical claims into their own views about whether it is possible to do nothing at all, the topic raised by *Let's Do Nothing*.

One other aim of the course is to assist students in deciphering texts that on first reading perplex them. Just as they received the message that all writing is rewriting, the idea that all reading is rereading receives repeated emphasis in this course. And one of the central skills for any philosophy student is the ability to articulate the argument put forward in a difficult philosophical text.

In order to succeed at this, students have to revise their notion of what reading a text requires. It is not something they can do while plugged into the latest hits they have downloaded from iTunes. Reading requires focused attention and has to be done more than once if the goal is to understand an argument well enough to formulate objections, regardless of how tentative both of those might be. So there are important lessons to be learned about reading philosophical works that students won't always assimilate without complaining.

Another issue is the difficulty students, especially first-year ones, have in criticizing the writing of one of their peers. It was also one that I was not sufficiently cognizant of in developing the course.

Perhaps because they have been socialized to be "nice," students initially have difficulty presenting significant criticisms of another student's work. It is crucial for them to realize that criticism is the bread and butter of the development of one's philosophical ideas.

It helps to share with them the difficulty one might have had early in one's career in accepting criticisms people made of one's writing. Explaining that now, after many years, one realizes that such criticisms are crucial to improving one's own thinking and writing, so that blandly positive responses to one's writing are now disappointing, for they do not provide any guidance for improving one's ideas.

It is counterproductive for the students to worry that they will hurt their classmates' feelings if they say that their work has problems in it. To help them see why, it is important for the instructor to make it clear that *they* are very likely to notice these weaknesses when they read the student's paper and penalize the writer of the essay for their presence. So the best way to help a classmate get a good grade (and also improve their philosophical thinking) is by showing them the weaknesses in their paper so that they have the opportunity to strengthen their argument.

Part of the problem was my not realizing that students need to be taught how to criticize their peers. This issue can be at least partially alleviated by discussing the importance of making helpful criticisms of a paper during the initial session(s) of the course.

When reading the professional philosophers, one thing students get taught to do is to formulate criticisms of the arguments advanced. Getting them to see that it is important to apply this evolving skill to their classmates' work is something that the instructor needs to emphasize.

A sports analogy is helpful here. If a student noticed that a teammate was not swinging their baseball bat correctly and thought that this was why they kept grounding out, it would be irresponsible not to tell them that they were making a mistake. Receiving such helpful feedback is the only way for them to improve.

The same holds for the "game" of philosophy. Philosophy is a complex activity that requires participants to possess a range of different skills. These include reading, abstracting ideas, criticizing views one understands, discussing one's opinions critically, writing an essay that presents and defends a view, listening to criticism, reformulating one's ideas in light of criticisms, responding to criticisms one thinks are misguided, etc.

Perhaps the most important of these skills is that of criticizing an argument made by another philosopher. In order to do this effectively, one not only has to criticize others' views, but also listen to and respond to criticisms of one's own. That's why critique plays such a big role in the picture-book introduction to philosophy course.

And that's why students have to make insightful criticisms of their peers. If the students see their own writing as an analogy of a baseball swing, something that they could improve in light of receiving helpful criticism, they become more capable of pointing out flaws in their classmates' papers.

It's also important to impress upon students that a criticism is not the last word. When Descartes's contemporaries criticized his claims in the *Meditations on First Philosophy*, he did not simply pack up shop. Rather, he *responded* to the criticisms in a series of *Replies* in which he explained to his critics what they had gotten wrong.

Students need to see that their classmates can have the sort of resiliency Descartes exhibited. Even if they are criticized, for example, for endorsing Moore's claim that they can't be mistaken about having two hands, they don't have to simply accept the criticism but can defend their view with a counterargument.

Just as a baseball team doesn't give up when their opponents score a run, philosophers don't give up their views simply because they have been subject to serious criticism. Defending a view against an apparently devastating criticism is a mark of good philosophical thinking.

It's not just philosophy that benefits when a student learns how to critique an argument. Having the ability to critique an argument is central to all learning, which requires a student to refine their views and respond to others' objections. All of the skills that the students learn in the picture-book introduction to philosophy course can be applied in *all* of their classes and, indeed, in much of their postcollege life.

Studying philosophy is, as Plato and others have maintained, an excellent guide for living one's life.

FINAL THOUGHTS

The Big Ideas for Little Kids Program introduced a subject matter often taken to be the sole province of college and university courses into the curricula of elementary schools through the use of picture books. The other chapters in this book have documented the great ingenuity that people have used to bring philosophical discussions into other contexts, such as working with younger kids or adults, using facilitators other than college students, even creating one's own picture books to address issues specific to a given situation.

The current chapter is a reversal of the strategy of the Big Ideas Program. It details an effort to incorporate some of the salient features of an elementary school philosophy class into a college-level introductory philosophy course.

Despite some difficulties encountered, the course has been very successful, with many of the students becoming very engaged in philosophy as a result of taking it. The students also forged close relationships with their peers from working so closely with them, and with their professor as well.

This chapter shows that the Big Ideas Program can even inspire its originator to transform his own college teaching by incorporating ideas and strategies originally formulated to allow young children to discuss philosophy. Big kids deserve the chance to talk about Big Ideas just as much as little kids do. The picture-book introduction to philosophy course is one way to allow them to do so.

NOTES

1. Thanks to Erik Kenyon for helpful comments on drafts of this chapter.
2. Keith Hjortshoj (2009, 59–64) emphasizes the importance of rewriting for students.

REFERENCES

Bain, Ken. 2004. *What the Best College Teachers Do*. Cambridge, MA: Harvard University Press.
Descartes, René. 2006. *Meditations, Objections, and Replies*. Translated by Roger Ariew and Donald Cress. Indianapolis, IN: Hackett.
Fucille, Tony. 1966. *Let's Do Nothing*. Somerville, MA: Candlewick Press.
Geisel, Theodore (Dr. Seuss). 1961. *The Sneetches*. New York: Random House.
Goldberg, David Theo. 1990. "Racism and Rationality: The Need for a New Critique." *Philosophy of the Social Sciences* 20, no. 3: 317–50.
Hjortshoj, Keith. 2009. *The Transition to College Writing.* 2nd edition. Boston and New York: Bedford / St. Martin's.
Johnson, Crockett. 2015. *Harold and the Purple Crayon*. New York: HarperCollins.
Kennett, Jeanette, and Michael Smith. 1996. "Frog and Toad Lose Control." *Analysis* 56, no. 2: 63–73.
Lobel, Arnold. 1979. *Frog and Toad Together*. New York: HarperCollins.

Moore, G. E. 1959. "A Defense of Common Sense." In *Philosophical Papers*. London: Allen & Unwin.
Nichols, Shaun. 2007. "Imagination and Immortality: The Thinking Me." *Synthese* 159, no. 2: 215–33.
Reynolds, Peter H. 2004. *Ish*. Somerville, MA: Candlewick Press.
Sartre, Jean-Paul. 1993. "The Origin of Negation." In *Being and Nothingness*. Translated by Hazel Barnes. New York: Washington Square Press.
Thurber, James. 1943. *Many Moons*. New York: Harcourt Brace.
Trelease, Jim. 2013. *The Read-Aloud Handbook*. 7th edition. New York: Penguin Books.
Tsanoff, Radoslav A. 1940. "The Notion of Perfection." *Philosophical Review* 49, no. 1: 25–36.
Wartenberg, Thomas. 2014. *Big Ideas for Little Kids: Teaching Philosophy through Children's Literature*. 2nd edition. Lanham, MD: Rowman & Littlefield.
———. 2013. *A Sneetch Is a Sneetch and Other Philosophical Discoveries: Finding Wisdom in Children's Literature*. Malden, MA: Wiley-Blackwell.

List of Contributors

Ali Bassiri is a physician and an MBA. He is a former member of the San Jose Rotary Club with a strong interest in both children's education and philosophy. Along with school principal Maria Evans, he created the Washington Elementary School Philosophy Project, which lasted from 2011 to 2013. He was the chairman of the O'Connor Hospital Bioethics Committee in San Jose from 2004 to 2006 and has been actively involved in bioethics throughout his clinical career from 1998 to present. He has two boys, ages seven and ten years old, with whom he enjoys sailing, hiking, playing the guitar, and, of course, philosophy.

Mitchell Bickman is the director of social studies in the Oceanside School District. He received his undergraduate degree in history and education from the University of Michigan, and his master of science in secondary education from Hofstra University. Mr. Bickman is the recipient of the 2016 New York State Social Studies Supervisory Association's (NYSCSS & NYS4A) Supervisor of the Year Award. This award is given to professionals who have demonstrated the highest commitment to social studies education in New York State and have established innovative and effective supervisory techniques.

Stephen L. Esquith is the dean of the residential college in the arts and humanities, Michigan State University. He is currently working on several local peace-building projects in Mali and similar peace-education projects for refugee children in Michigan. He has been a Fulbright Scholar in Poland and in Mali and is the author of *Intimacy and Spectacle* (Cornell, 1994), *The Political Responsibilities of Everyday Bystanders* (Pennsylvania State University Press, 2010), and numerous articles, most recently on children's human rights, democratic political education, and humanitarian assistance. He has taught Philosophy for Children in middle schools in Michigan and Mali over the past fifteen years.

Daniel Groll is an associate professor in the philosophy department at Carleton College in Northfield, Minnesota. In addition to teaching Philosophy with Children, Daniel routinely teaches in normative ethics, medical ethics, and family ethics. His research focuses on issues related to, and arising from, decision making and interpersonal disagreement. He has published papers on moral disagreement, paternalism, medical decision making, and moral testimony. He is currently working on a project on the ethics of gamete donation and the value, if any, of having knowledge of one's genetic origins.

Erik Kenyon holds a PhD in classics from Cornell University (2012) with a focus in ancient philosophy. His book *Augustine and the Dialogue* (Cambridge University Press, 2018) explores philosophy of education and the dialogue form in Augustine's earliest works. He has taught at Rollins College since 2012, with courses in classics, philosophy, and humanities. In 2016 he became director of Student and Faculty Engagement for Rollins's evening school, where he organizes adjunct faculty development and a lifelong learning program for senior citizens. Kenyon's Philosophy for Kids courses have worked with six Orlando-area schools, partnering undergraduates with children from three to twelve years old. Working with Diane Doyle and Sharon Carnahan of Rollins's Child Development and Student Resource Center, he has coauthored two articles on pre-K philosophy and *Ethics for the Very Young: A Philosophical Curriculum for Early Childhood Education* (Rowman & Littlefield, 2019).

Stephen Kekoa Miller has taught philosophy and religious studies at Oakwood Friends School and Marist College in Poughkeepsie, New York, for eighteen years. Stephen is the president of the United Nations Association Mid-Hudson Valley chapter. Stephen is also the treasurer and member of the board of directors of PLATO (Philosophy Learning and Teaching Organization). Stephen speaks and publishes in the areas of Philosophy for Children, philosophy of emotions, ethics education, and virtue ethics. Stephen also serves on the Teachers Advisory Council of the National Humanities Center and the Ethics Board of the Town of Poughkeepsie.

Laura Trongard is a National Board–certified high school teacher in Oceanside, New York. She graduated summa cum laude from Hofstra University with a bachelor of arts degree in history and also completed a master of science in secondary education at Hofstra University. Mrs. Trongard teaches AP world history, AP United States government and politics, economics, and a mentoring course. She has been recognized as a 2016 Collaborator of Excellence by the New York State English Council for her work relating to the philosophy program in Oceanside.

Thomas E. Wartenberg, a senior research fellow in philosophy at Mount Holyoke College, has published numerous books and articles, including *Big Ideas for Little Kids: Teaching Philosophy Through Children's Literature* (Rowman & Littlefield, 2nd edition, 2014), and *A Sneetch Is a Sneetch and Other Philosophical Discoveries: Finding Wisdom in Children's Literature* (Wiley-Blackwell, 2013). The program that he founded, Teaching Children Philosophy (www.teachingchildrenphilosophy.org), was awarded the 2011 APA/PDC Prize for Excellence and Innovations in Philosophy Programs. He received the 2013 Merritt Prize for his contributions to the philosophy of education. His Philosophy for Children course is the subject of a PBS documentary: http://wgby.org/bigideas. His other publications include *Mel Bochner: Illustrating Philosophy* (MHCMA, 2015), *Existentialism: A Beginner's Guide* (Oneworld, 2008), *Thinking on Screen: Film as Philosophy* (Routledge, 2007), and *Unlikely Couples: Movie Romance and Social Criticism* (Westview, 1999). He served as president of PLATO (Philosophy Learning and Teaching Organization) from 2016 to 2018.

and teaches [illegible] theory [illegible] governance and politi[illegible] [illegible] [illegible] [illegible] [illegible] [illegible] [illegible] [illegible] [illegible]

Thulin [illegible] [illegible] [illegible] [illegible] [illegible] [illegible] [illegible] [illegible] Philosophy [illegible] [illegible] [illegible] [illegible] [illegible] [illegible] [illegible] [illegible] [illegible] [illegible] philosophy [illegible] [illegible] [illegible] serve[illegible] [illegible] [illegible] [illegible] [illegible] served as president [illegible] [illegible] [illegible] from 2010 to 2013.

www.ingramcontent.com/pod-product-compliance
Lightning Source LLC
Chambersburg PA
CBHW051814230426
43672CB00012B/2728